A Young Person's Guide To

MUSIC

A Young Person's Guide To

MUSIC

Neil Ardley with Music by Poul Ruders

In association with the BBC Symphony Orchestra
conducted by Andrew Davis

DK

DK

LONDON, NEW YORK, MUNICH,
MELBOURNE AND DELHI

Project editor Claire Gillard
Art editor Neville Graham
Editor Phil Wilkinson
US editor Mary Sutherland
Designer Kati Poynor
Managing editor Gillian Denton
Managing art editor Julia Harris
Production Catherine Semark
Picture research Giselle Harvey
Photography Steve Gorton,
Susanna Price,
Andy Crawford
Consultant Susan Sturrock

First published in the United States in 1995
This edition published in the United States in 2004

by Dorling Kindersley Publishing, Inc.,
375 Hudson St., New York, NY 10014

Library of Congress Cataloging-in-Publication Data

Ardley, Neil.
A young person's guide to music / by Neil Ardley.
p. cm. + 1 sound cassette
Includes index.
Contents: pt. 1. Making music -- pt. 2. The history of music.
ISBN 0 7566 0540 7
1. Music--Instruction and study. 2. Orchestra. 3. Music--History and criticism.
MT6.A73Y68 1995
780--dc20   95-19595
CIP
MN

Color reproduction by Colourscan, Singapore
Printed in China by Toppan Printing Co. (Shenzen) Ltd.

Find out more at
www.dk.com

Contents

The compact disc

THE BBC commissioned Danish composer Poul Ruders to write a work to commemorate two musical anniversaries: the 300th anniversary of the death of English composer Henry Purcell and the 50th anniversary of Benjamin Britten's composition of *A Young Person's Guide to the Orchestra*, based on a theme by Purcell. The resulting work is *Concerto in Pieces*. It is in the form of a set of variations on the *Witches' Chorus* from Purcell's opera *Dido and Aeneas*. Each of the ten variations highlights different groups of instruments, so that the whole work gives a vivid picture of the many different faces of the symphony orchestra. After the performance of the concerto, conductor Andrew Davis "takes the concerto to pieces," describing the main themes and combinations of instruments, and illustrating them with excerpts from the work.

Poul Ruders
Concerto in Pieces
(Purcell Variations for Orchestra)

BBC Symphony Orchestra conducted by Andrew Davis

1	Theme	
2–3	Variation I	*Vivace maestoso*
4–5	Variation II	*Vivace scherzando*
6	Variation III	*Parlando alla breve*
7–12	Variation IV	*Largo recitativo*
13–15	Variation V	*Allegretto capriccioso*
16–20	Variation VI	*Martellato feroce*
21–23	Variation VII	*Andante lamentoso*
24–25	Variation VIII	*Adagio lontano*
26	Variation IX	*Intermezzo*
27–33	Variation X	*Finale fugato vivace*

34   Taking the Concerto to Pieces
Andrew Davis explains the inspiration and construction of *Concerto in Pieces*

MUSICAL INDEX

STRINGS	WOODWINDS	BRASS	PERCUSSION	KEYBOARDS
35 violin	41 flute	51 trumpet	55 cymbals	61 piano
36 viola	42 piccolo	52 tuba	56 timpani	62 celesta
37 cello	43 clarinet	53 horn	57 tam-tam	63 harpsichord
38 double bass	44 bass clarinet	54 trombone	58 tubular bells	64 organ
39 harp	45 oboe		59 glockenspiel	65 synthesizer
40 guitar	46 English horn		60 vibraphone	
	47 bassoon			
	48 contrabassoon			
	49 saxophone			
	50 recorder			

Recorded at BBC Studios, Maida Vale, London, on 31 May 1995
Recording producer: Ann McKay
Recording engineer: Neil Pemberton
Sound editing: Philip Ashley
Synthesizer sampling: Gert Sørensen, Copenhagen
℗1995 BBC
Music published by Edition Wilhelm Hansen AS
This recording is exclusively licensed to Dorling Kindersley Limited

Spoken narrative © 1995 Dorling Kindersley Limited, London
Musical Index compiled by Guy Dagul
Extracts from Purcell's *Dido and Aeneas*
© 1990 The Decca Record Company Limited, London (425 720-2)

STEREO DDD
Compact disc manufactured by General C.D. Pte Limited, Singapore

How to use this book and compact disc

THE BOOK AND accompanying CD are designed to be used together. Many of the pages, especially those discussing instruments, feature CD symbols that show which track of the CD to listen to when you are reading the text. The book has two parts; the first part explains how music is made and the second part deals with the history of classical music.

Selecting a track

The CD listening symbols indicate which track to play for each instrument or orchestral section. Key in the track number or use the track selection buttons on the CD player. Then press PLAY to listen to the track.

CD listening symbol

Track number

Length of track in minutes and seconds

Part one
Making music

This part of the book describes the orchestra, the roles of the conductor and composer, and musical instruments. It shows how the instruments work, how they are played, what sort of sounds they make, and their role in the orchestra.

Introduction
Each "family" of instruments is introduced here. The sound and general features of the family are described

How the instruments work
This text describes the basic workings of the family of instruments, showing how their sound is made

Diagrams
These drawings help to explain how the instruments work

Captions
These give the basic facts about each instrument

CD listening symbols
These show which track on the CD illustrates each instrument

Annotations
These point to different parts of the instrument and describe what they do

Part two
The history of music

This part of the book tells the story of classical music, from the earliest times to today. It contains timelines, an A–Z of composers, a section on musical forms, and a glossary.

Introduction
An introduction outlines the most important musical developments in each period

Timeline
The timeline itself runs beneath the five-line staff, which flows in a continuous curve across the page

The changing world
To set the music in its context, some of the most significant historical events are listed in this box

Music titles
A title in *italics* is a particular name given to a work, usually by the composer.

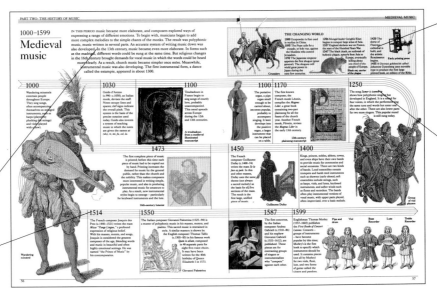

7

Pianist   Trumpeter   Cellist   Flautist   Horn player

PART ONE

MAKING MUSIC

THE COMPACT DISC that comes with this book begins with the sound of the full symphony orchestra – almost 100 people making music together. The sound of the orchestra is exhilarating. It can be majestic or moving, joyful or sad. It can even make you want to dance or to sing along with the music. The first part of the book explores the orchestra – its instruments, where the different players sit, the role of the conductor and leader, and how they all work together to express the spirit of the composer's music. It also describes the way in which composers work – what makes them write music in the first place, and how they turn their ideas into an orchestral composition that musicians can perform.

As the music on the CD continues, the orchestra splits up into various groups of instruments – strings, woodwinds, brass, and percussion – and individual players also have their own solo passages. The book treats each instrument separately within its group or family, showing how it works and produces sounds, and how people play different instruments to make music.

These instruments are not only played in orchestras. They also make great music on their own, and small groups of musicians can get together to play chamber music, such as piano trios, string quartets, and wind quintets. For some instruments, such as the piano and violin, there is a huge amount of solo and chamber music. For others, like the percussion instruments, there is much less. An indication of the range of music available for each instrument is also given.

Making music is fun. Whether you play in a large orchestra, a small chamber group, or on your own, music offers a world of interest and enjoyment.

CD listening symbol

Violinist

Timpanist

Oboist

Harpist

Clarinetist

Trombonist

The orchestra

THE LARGEST GROUP of musicians that performs classical music is the orchestra. Orchestras exist to play the huge variety of orchestral music written by composers over the last four centuries. They mostly perform famous works of the past, but modern composers like Poul Ruders continue to explore new ways of making sounds using the orchestral medium.

One of the most exciting musical experiences is to hear the rich sound of a full orchestra. Play the CD that comes with this book and listen to a leading orchestra performing Poul Ruders' *Concerto in Pieces*, a showpiece for the hundred or so musicians in the orchestra. From its opening theme to the tremendous climax at the end, the instruments combine in many different ways to produce a dazzling array of sounds.

Keeping an orchestra
Orchestras were first heard almost 400 years ago in opera houses. Kings and nobles also kept orchestras for performances at court. The French king Louis XIV was able to provide his court composer Lully with a large number of musicians, enabling Lully to develop the sound of the orchestra. Today, the best orchestras are maintained by large cities and national broadcasting organizations.

The BBC Symphony Orchestra

This is the orchestra that performs *Concerto in Pieces*. It is the principal orchestra of the British Broadcasting Corporation, and is based in London. It is called a "symphony" orchestra because many of the works it plays are symphonies, but the orchestra also performs many other kinds of music. This size of orchestra is standard for music composed over the last 100 years.

The percussionists, who may each play several instruments, sit or stand at the back

An orchestra normally contains one or two harps, usually placed on the left

The violinists sit in several rows at the front and to the left of the orchestra

Extra forces

The number of musicians in the orchestra may vary greatly from one piece of music to the next. Most orchestral music composed about two centuries ago requires around 30 players, whereas some music of the late 19th and 20th centuries calls for more than 100 musicians. An orchestra employs a core number of musicians who play in most performances. Extra players are hired for works needing larger forces, as in this performance by the BBC Symphony Orchestra of the *Turangalîla Symphony* by Messiaen, in which his wife, Yvonne Loriod, plays an unusual electronic instrument called the ondes martenot.

10 percussionists play a wide range of instruments, including the glockenspiel and vibraphone

Celesta   30 violins

PLAY TRACKS 1 AND 2

"The concerto opens with the glorious sound of the full orchestra playing Purcell's witches' theme; at track 2, the first variation begins, in which parts of the original theme are played by all the instruments in full cry."

The central block of players contains two rows of woodwinds and, behind them, a row of horns

Trumpeters, trombonists, and the tuba player all sit at the back

The musicians in the center and at the sides and back of the orchestra are raised on tiers so that they can see the conductor easily

The double basses are placed to the right

This violinist is the concertmaster of the orchestra

The conductor stands on a platform called a rostrum to direct the orchestra

The violas and cellos are arranged in several rows at the front and to the right of the orchestra

11 woodwinds

13 brass instruments

8 double basses

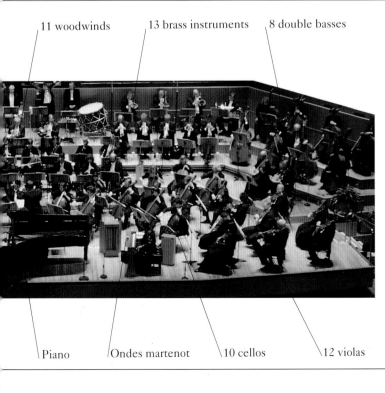

Piano

Ondes martenot

10 cellos

12 violas

Orchestras large and small

The size of an orchestra usually reflects the type of music it performs. Some small orchestras play only early music, which requires relatively few players. Symphony orchestras often add a large choir to perform choral works.

Authentic orchestra
This orchestra specializes in playing early music. There is no conductor, and the players use old instruments to recreate the sounds of an 18th century orchestra.

Augmented orchestra
Choral works such as masses and requiems require a large choir or chorus in addition to the orchestra. Many orchestras have their own choir.

The four sections

Orchestras may vary greatly in size, but they all contain four main sections of instruments – strings, woodwinds, brass, and percussion. The members of the orchestra sit in a semicircle around the conductor, with the strings – instruments with the softest sounds – at the front. In the center, behind the strings, are the woodwinds, the next softest-sounding group. The brass and percussion – the loudest sections of the orchestra – sit or stand at the sides and along the back.

The percussion section

The percussion instruments are arranged in a line at the back of the orchestra, giving the players room to move from one instrument to another. The percussion section may include drums, cymbals, triangle, gongs, glockenspiel, and xylophone.

Multiple roles

One percussionist usually plays a set of timpani, or kettledrums (below), while the others each play about three or four different percussion instruments (left).

PLAY TRACK 19

"The battering drums and gongs of the percussion section transform the mood of mockery in the original witches' chorus into one of sheer ferocity and terror."

PLAY TRACK 8

"Beginning with high violins followed by lower violas, and finally deep cellos and double basses, the strings build up a huge celestial chord. By bowing slowly back and forth, the strings can hold this chord for a long time."

The string section

Five groups of players make up the string section – two groups of violins called first violins and second violins, violas, cellos, and double basses. The number of string players can vary without affecting the music because the players in each group all play the same notes. However, a large number of players is needed in each group to produce a good string sound, and an orchestra usually has a combined force of about 60 string players.

First and second violins

The violins are positioned to the left of the conductor. The first violins sit closest to the audience, with the second violins behind them. The first and second violins each play a different musical line.

Violas and cellos

Here, the violas are to the right of the conductor and closest to the audience with the cellos behind. The positions of the cellos and violas can be reversed.

Second winds
One of a group of woodwind players of the same instrument often doubles on or plays a second instrument. For example, one of three flautists may also play the piccolo (see above), one oboist may also play the English horn, one clarinetist can double on the bass clarinet or saxophone, and one bassoonist may also play the contrabassoon.

The woodwind section
Flutes, oboes, clarinets, and bassoons make up the woodwind section, usually in pairs or groups of three players. The woodwind players normally sit in two rows – the flutes and oboes make up the front row, with the clarinets and bassoons behind them.

PLAY TRACK 4
"The second variation starts to break up the witches' theme – it is like seeing it through a distorting mirror. The woodwinds toss bits of the theme to and fro, making a musical line that moves through all the registers of the woodwinds."

The brass section
The standard brass section contains four horns, three trumpets, three trombones, and one tuba. The brass players sometimes insert mutes into the bells of their instruments, which softens the sound and changes the tone.

PLAY TRACK 6
"The brass begin the third variation, with the horns, trumpets, and trombones each playing pairs of notes in turn. When subdued, brass instruments all have a mellow quality that demonstrates the kinship in sound between them."

A line of horns
The horn players usually sit in a line near the back of the orchestra. They are apart from the other brass instruments because they often play a different line of music.

Trumpets, trombones, and tuba
These brass instruments are situated at the back and toward the right of the orchestra. The players sit in a line, or in two rows with the trumpeters at the front.

Double basses
The double bass players stand, or sit on high stools, behind the violas.

The conductor

A GREAT ORCHESTRAL performance results when the musical feelings that the composer puts into a piece of music are expressed as strongly as possible by the orchestra. The overall responsibility for this lies in the hands of the conductor. Because orchestral music involves so many people – not only the orchestra but often soloists, singers, and even choirs – the conductor is required to direct the performance. Standing on a central rostrum, or raised platform, in order to be easily visible to all players, and using hand and arm gestures, body movements, and facial expressions, the conductor controls and evaluates the sound of the orchestra, and strives to draw from the musicians as powerful a performance as possible – one that will move the audience. An orchestra usually appoints a principal conductor, who works mainly with that orchestra and directs most of their concerts.

Interpreting a piece

Many conductors direct a piece of music as the composer intended it to be played. Others create their own individual interpretation of the music. The composer Igor Stravinsky (right) wanted his music to retain its own special character, and wrote it with exact instructions on how the music should be performed.

At rehearsal

A conductor's work begins with a study of the musical score. He or she learns the music, and gets to know exactly how it will sound when it is played. Shortly before the performance, the conductor rehearses the music with the orchestra. He or she explains to the players how the music is to be performed, and they play through the piece, stopping to work on tricky passages. The conductor listens to make sure that each section plays at the correct volume to create a good blend of sounds.

The concertmaster

The conductor discusses the music with Michael Davis, the concertmaster of the BBC Symphony Orchestra. The concertmaster is the principal member of the first violins, and he or she conveys the conductor's intentions to the string section. These may be technical matters, or points of interpretation.

The soloist

Works such as concertos feature solo performers with the orchestra. The soloist has his or her own way of playing or singing the music, and the conductor has to direct the orchestra to support and follow the soloist's interpretation of the music. Here, the Brazilian cellist Antonio Meneses discusses a point with Andrew Davis during a rehearsal of Elgar's cello concerto.

In performance

Having dealt with technical and other matters at rehearsals, the conductor's role in a live concert, a recording, or a broadcast is to draw from the orchestra a powerful and moving performance of the music.

The right hand shows *when* things happen, and may set the tempo, or speed, of the music

Andrew Davis

The principal conductor of the BBC Symphony Orchestra, Andrew Davis, conducts the music that accompanies this book. As he conducts, the musicians watch him for signs that indicate how he wants them to play the music. He uses body movements and facial expressions to communicate how fast or slow, loud or soft, or in which mood to play the music. In this way he shapes the music into a special performance.

The baton

A white baton held in the right hand helps the orchestra to see the conductor's hand movements.

The facial expression reinforces the message given by the left hand

The left hand indicates *how* to play passages – here, with precision and clarity

The white baton is clearly visible to the whole orchestra

Ready, steady . . .
The conductor is about to start the music. The hands are poised to give the first signal, and he gives the orchestra a look of encouragement.

Hands poised to begin

Facial expression strengthens message given by left hand

Softly, softly
The left hand is held in front of the mouth to indicate that a passage should be played quietly.

Delicately, please
The conductor looks across to the first violins, his expression showing that he wants them to play with delicacy.

Conductor looks toward first violins

The composer

CLASSICAL MUSIC IS created by composers and played or sung by performers. This system has produced many masterpieces that, because they were written down by their composers, can still be played today and will continue to entertain and move listeners far into the future. Composers write music because they wish to express their musical feelings. But there are many different reasons why a composer begins a particular work.

Like many modern pieces of music, the work on the accompanying CD was commissioned. When a work is commissioned, a person or organization asks a composer to write a new piece, and pays the composer a fee. In this case, the British Broadcasting Corporation commissioned the Danish composer Poul Ruders to write a piece to mark the 300th anniversary of the death of the great English composer Henry Purcell. *Concerto in Pieces* is the result.

The 17th-century English composer Henry Purcell, whose opera *Dido and Aeneas* provides the theme for *Concerto in Pieces* by Poul Ruders

Engraving of firework display in London in 1749

Celebrating important events

Grand occasions demand grand music, and composers often write a piece to mark an important event. One of the best known is the *Music for the Royal Fireworks* (often known simply as the *Fireworks Music*) by Handel. This was composed for the official London celebration in 1749 of the Peace of Aix-la-Chapelle, which ended an eight-year war in Europe. The celebration included a magnificent firework display, for which Handel wrote the accompanying music. The work was originally performed by a large wind band, including 24 oboes and 12 bassoons, because the king, George II, wanted a "military" sound and disliked stringed instruments. The music became so popular that it has been played ever since in an arrangement for a normal orchestra with strings as well as woodwinds.

Sacred music

Many composers write music to express their religious beliefs. This was a common reason for writing music in the past, and most music composed before 1750 was religious in inspiration. Many sacred works are musical settings of church services, like the Mass, and such works are often performed in churches as well as concert halls. A famous modern sacred work is the *War Requiem* composed by Britten in 1961. This work is a memorial for those killed in war, and was written for its first performance in the rebuilt Coventry Cathedral, England. This building was destroyed during World War II, and the *War Requiem* marked the consecration of the new cathedral.

The new Coventry Cathedral, built next to the ruins of the old

Composing for gifted performers

Composers often write pieces for a particular performer. This may happen because the performer commissions a new work or because the composer has a favorite player in mind. In either case, the special performer normally gives the work's first performance, after which it is made available to anyone capable of playing it. Such works can show off the performer's virtuosity and develop the scope of their instrument. A performer who has had several new works written for him is the Swedish musician Håkan Hardenberger, one of today's foremost trumpet players. The conductor Paul Sacher commissioned the work *Endless Parade*, by Harrison Birtwistle, for Hardenberger. Peter Maxwell Davies, Hans Werner Henze, and Toru Takemitsu have also composed concertos for him.

King William III   Queen Mary

Trumpeter
Håkan
Hardenberger

Harrison Birtwistle
wrote *Endless
Parade* for
trumpet,
vibraphone,
and strings

Royal entertainment

In the past, kings and nobles often employed composers to write music that would entertain them and their guests. Henry Purcell composed much music for English monarchs William III and Queen Mary. He composed music to entertain them at court on occasions such as royal birthdays, or to welcome the royal family back to court after visits elsewhere. A famous modern musical entertainment is *Façade* by Walton. This is a setting of witty poems by writer Edith Sitwell for reader and six musicians. It was written in 1922 to entertain the poet's family, but it soon became popular; a ballet and two orchestral suites based on the music were produced.

A scene from the film *The Piano*

Commercial music

A huge amount of music, such as jingles for television ads and film music, is written for commercial reasons. The music has to support what is seen on the screen and, to achieve this, a commercial composer has to be able to write music to order in many different styles. Music contributes greatly to the atmosphere of a film, and a film producer may choose a particular composer because their kind of music will suit the film. One example is *The Piano*, a film with piano music composed by Michael Nyman.

The French
emperor Napoleon

The composer's inspiration

Often composers write a piece of music for no particular reason but from sheer inspiration. The composer's imagination can be triggered by anything – a musical theme, or something outside music, such as a person the composer admires or loves. For example, Beethoven originally wrote his Third Symphony as a tribute to Napoleon Bonaparte, whom he admired as a heroic leader. But Beethoven was an antiroyalist, and when Napoleon crowned himself emperor, the composer was outraged. Beethoven removed the dedication to Napoleon and called the work *Sinfonia Eroica (Heroic Symphony)*. This name has lived on ever since.

The manuscript of
Beethoven's *Eroica*,
with Napoleon's
name scratched out

The composer at work

COMPOSERS CREATE MUSIC in different ways. Some can write down music just as it comes into their heads; other composers prefer to sit at the piano and play musical ideas that occur to them before writing them down on paper. Composers also differ in the way they organize their musical thoughts. Some jot down musical ideas that inspire them at any time, and later use these ideas when a new work is required. Another approach is to plan the overall structure of the work at the very beginning, so that the music has a good framework as it is composed. A composer may draw inspiration from the music of an earlier composer, and might even take his or her style and method of composing as a starting point for their own work. A composer will sometimes base a new work on an existing theme or group of notes from another composer's work, reshaping this material in various ways to develop a very different piece. Poul Ruders began *Concerto in Pieces* by basing it on the fast *Witches' Chorus* from the famous opera *Dido and Aeneas* by Purcell. He then planned and developed ten variations on this original theme, combining different groups of instruments in each variation to demonstrate the diversity of sound of the symphony orchestra.

A Scene from Purcell's *Dido and Aeneas*

The composer tries out a passage and pencils it on to the page

Sketching a rough draft

Poul Ruders works at the piano because he likes to hear the music as he composes it. He writes a rough draft, or sketch, of the music on large sheets of music paper, noting the names of the instruments that are to play. As he tries out the music on the piano, Poul can imagine the sounds of the different orchestral instruments playing the notes. He erases or crosses out any passages that do not work.

Rough sketch of *Concerto in Pieces*
This is the sketch of the ending. The notes will reappear, in a revised and expanded form, in the final version.

Writing the score

When the sketch of a work is finished, the composer writes a complete copy of the piece, called the score. This contains the music for all the different instruments of the orchestra, and will be used by the conductor of the work. Poul Ruders writes the score away from the piano, so that he can concentrate on what the sounds of the instruments will be like when the music is performed. Referring closely to the sketch, he writes a separate line of music for each instrument. He may change some of the notes at this stage. The notes on this score are later keyed into a computer, and the completed score is printed.

Poul Ruders completing the score of *Concerto in Pieces*

PLAY TRACK 33

"I use the full orchestra to bring the concerto to a triumphant ending with everyone playing a crescendo that erupts into the final gigantic chord."

The finished score

This is the final page of the hand-written score of *Concerto in Pieces*. The layout of instruments is standard, with woodwinds at the top, followed by the brass, percussion, harp, piano, and strings at the bottom. Poul Ruders has changed the music slightly, making the final crescendo last only two bars, instead of four bars in the sketch.

The instrumental parts

The players in the orchestra do not play from the score. Instead, each musician has a part that contains only the music for that particular instrument. The computer extracts the part from the full score and prints it out. This is the last page of the double bass part.

Taking the concerto to pieces

POUL RUDERS' NEW composition combines two musical forms. It is a concerto for orchestra, which displays the composer's skill in writing music for the orchestra and the musicians' ability to play it. The work is also a theme and variations, each variation being a piece of the whole composition, hence the title *Concerto in Pieces*. All composers build a work using basic musical elements – melody, harmony, counterpoint, and rhythm. A composer must combine these elements skillfully if the music is to sound convincing. Orchestral composition demands a thorough knowledge of all the instruments of the orchestra. The composer must be aware of the limitations of each instrument in order to write music that all the players will be able to perform without difficulty.

The theme
This is the first page of the printed score, which contains the theme. At the top is the Italian instruction *Vivace Maestoso*, which means "lively and majestic," followed by the tempo, or speed, marking of 120 beats per minute. The staffs are labeled with the Italian names of the instruments. Each staff also has the time signature 9/8, which indicates the basic rhythm of the music – nine beats to the measure, and the eighth note gets the beat.

Counterpoint
The composer writes two or more melodies or parts, and combines them so that they are heard together. This combining of melodies to produce a pleasant harmony is known as counterpoint. *Concerto in Pieces* opens with the original theme by Purcell, which is in four-part counterpoint. The first part is played by the horns, second violins, and violas; the second by the English horn and saxophone; the third by the oboes, trumpets, and first violins; and the fourth by the bass clarinet, bassoons, and cellos.

Woodwinds
Brass
Percussion
Harp/keyboards
Strings

PLAY TRACK 1
"The opening theme is in four-part counterpoint, just as in Purcell's Witches' Chorus, *with different instrumental groups playing each of the four musical lines."*

CONCERTO IN PIECES
(Purcell–Variations)

Theme

Poul Ruders, 1995

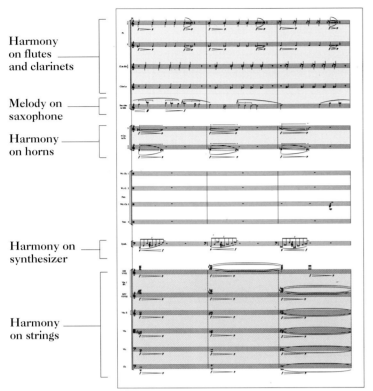

Harmony on flutes and clarinets

Melody on saxophone

Harmony on horns

Harmony on synthesizer

Harmony on strings

Melody and harmony

A tune or theme is a melody, and consists of a single line of notes. The instruments playing the melody are usually accompanied by other instruments. The sound produced by the accompanying instruments as their notes combine with those of the melody is called the harmony. Harmony helps to create feelings such as joy or sadness in music. Changing harmonies also helps the music to flow and develop, adding depth to the music.

PLAY TRACK 12

"The saxophone plays a singing melody over a harmony provided by flutes, clarinets, horns, synthesizer, and strings. The chords in the harmony alternate between minor and major as the melody progresses."

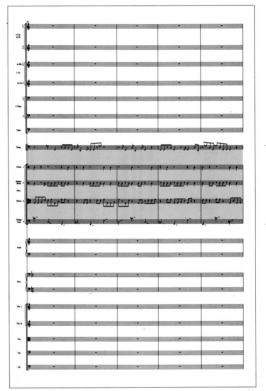

Rhythmic pattern on timpani, marching drum, and roto-toms; basic beat on gongs and bass drum

Rhythm and tempo

The length or duration of each note determines the rhythm of the music. By using sequences of different-length notes, the composer creates different rhythmic patterns. Rhythm is different from the tempo of the music, which is how quickly or slowly the music is played. The mood of the music depends greatly on its rhythm and tempo. Fast rhythmic patterns can give the music life and make it dance.

Sound of Purcell orchestra on flutes, piccolo, oboes, and bassoon

"Yapping" sound on muted horns, trumpets, and trombones

Melody given to tuba

Sound of Purcell orchestra on second violins and double basses

PLAY TRACK 20

"Over a basic beat on the gongs and deep bass drum, the other drums play more complex rhythms that all combine to drive the music along with terrific energy."

Orchestration

When the composer has written the notes of the music using the basic elements of melody, harmony, counterpoint, and rhythm, he or she chooses instruments or voices to play or sing the notes. This selection of particular instruments or voices makes a big difference to the overall sound and the effect of the music on the listener. A composer like Poul Ruders can produce a very individual sound from the orchestra.

PLAY TRACK 14

"The tuba plays the melody in the fifth variation, while the original theme reappears on a few woodwinds and strings – they recreate the sound of an orchestra of Purcell's time. Behind these sounds can be heard a weird 'yapping' from muted brass."

Stringed instruments

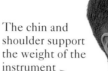

T HE NAME, stringed instruments, comes from strings that are stretched tightly over the instrument's body. The player draws a bow across the strings, or plucks the strings with the fingers, in order to produce a sound. Four instruments – the violin, viola, cello (or violoncello), and double bass – make up the orchestral string family. These are usually played with a bow, enabling the strings to produce expressive sounds. All orchestras have a string section, most chamber music is written for strings, and there is a lot of solo music for the violin and cello. Other stringed instruments, including the guitar and harp, are played by plucking the strings.

How stringed instruments work

Bowing or plucking the strings makes them vibrate, and each vibrating string produces a different range of notes. The pitch of a note – how high or low it sounds – depends on the length, thickness or weight, and tension (tightness) of the string.

Length
Moving a finger up the string shortens the length that vibrates, and the note gets higher. Moving it down the string makes the note lower.

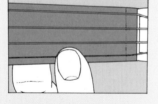

Thickness or weight
The strings differ in thickness or weight. A thick or heavy string vibrates more slowly than a thin or light string of the same length, producing a deeper note.

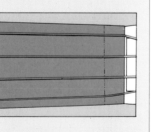

Tension
Tightening a string makes it vibrate more quickly, producing a higher note, while loosening it lowers the note. The tuning pegs adjust the tension.

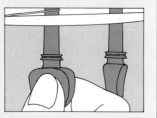

The violin

The smallest instrument of the string family, the violin produces the highest notes and has a singing tone. The violinist holds the instrument under the chin.

PLAY TRACK 6

"The high, slow notes above the brass and piano are played by violins, without vibrato, to create a mood of remoteness."

The chin and shoulder support the weight of the instrument

The left hand moves up and down the fingerboard, pressing down the strings to change the pitch

The bow is lightly held so the wrist is flexible for long sweeping arm movements or short, fast strokes

The viola

Like the violin, the viola is held under the chin. It is larger than the violin, and gives lower, more somber notes with a mellow tone.

PLAY TRACK 5

"Listen carefully, and you'll hear the violas playing soft echoing notes beneath the scurrying woodwinds."

The double bass

The largest instrument of the string family, the double bass is played standing up or sitting on a high stool. The player often plucks the strings to give a different sound.

PLAY TRACK 17

"The sixth variation begins with percussive sounds from the double basses and piano on opposite sides of the orchestra."

The cello

Larger than the violin and viola, the cello produces deep notes with a warm tone. The cellist sits while playing.

PLAY TRACK 25

"The weird noise that violently interrupts this spooky variation is produced by the cellos – instead of bowing, the players hit the strings with the wooden back of the bow."

The cellist's fingers have farther to travel up and down the cello's long fingerboard than the violinist's

Two notes can be played at once by drawing the bow across two adjacent strings

The bass's sloping shoulders make it easier for the left hand to reach the lower part of the fingerboard

This instrument has four strings, but some double basses have five strings

A mute clipped over the bridge muffles the tone of the strings

A steel pin or spike holds the weight of the instrument

String playing

THE VIOLIN IS representative of the whole string family in its construction and also in the way it makes its sound. The fingers of the left hand press the strings down on the fingerboard, while the right hand guides the bow smoothly over the strings, often changing direction without a break in the sound. Such skill requires a lot of practice. Moving the bow very quickly back and forth across the strings gives a quivering effect called *tremolo*.

Pizzicato
Plucking the strings with the fingers or thumb of the right hand is called *pizzicato*.

The chin rest allows the head and shoulder to grip the violin firmly

The strings' vibrations pass through the bridge and into the hollow body, which also vibrates to produce a rich sound

The bow is placed on the strings between the bridge and the end of the fingerboard

The f-shaped soundholes help the belly to vibrate, which amplifies the sound

A thin strip of wood called purfling strengthens the body and is also decorative

The narrowed waist of the violin allows the player to move the bow across the outer strings more easily

Family of bows

All bows consist of strands of horsehair or nylon stretched between the tip or head of the wooden stick and the nut, or frog, under the hand. A screw mechanism moves the nut to tighten or loosen the strands. The size of the bow varies according to the size of instrument. The double bass has the shortest and heaviest bow, with thicker strands of horsehair, and the violin has the longest bow of all.

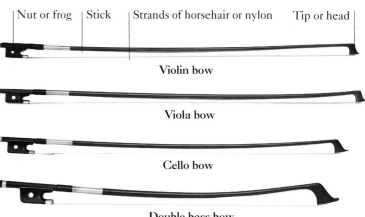

| Nut or frog | Stick | Strands of horsehair or nylon | Tip or head |

Violin bow

Viola bow

Cello bow

Double bass bow

Inside the body

The body is hollow and made of various kinds of springy wood that vibrate well. A long bass bar glued under the belly and a soundpost placed between the belly and the back carry vibrations from the bridge throughout the body so that the whole instrument rings with sound.

The parts of a violin

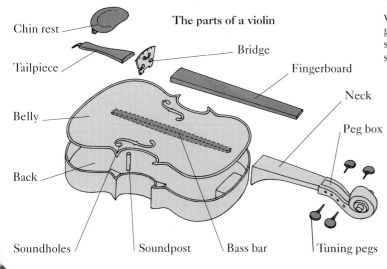

Chin rest

Tailpiece

Bridge

Fingerboard

Belly

Neck

Peg box

Back

Soundholes   Soundpost   Bass bar   Tuning pegs

The body is coated in varnish to protect the wood and to make it shine

The four strings are made of metal, or a core of gut or plastic around which thin metal wire is wound to give weight

The fingers change the lengths of the strings on the fingerboard, which is often made of dark ebony

With practice, the player learns the exact position of the fingers for each note

Sticky strings
The strands of the bow are rubbed with rosin. Usually made from the gum of pine trees, rosin makes the strands sticky so that they grip the string and cause it to vibrate.

Early ancestor

Viols are stringed instruments that were replaced by the violin, viola, cello, and double bass about 300 years ago. Most have six strings, and the fingerboard has frets like a guitar to show where to place the fingers. All viols are held upright, and the bow is held from below. They have a thinner sound than the violin and other strings, but are still used to perform early music.

Before starting, the player turns the tuning pegs to set each string to a certain pitch. Each string is called by its tuning pitch. The top string on a violin is called the E-string

The neck of the violin is carved with an ornamental scroll

Virtuoso violinist
The Israeli-born violinist, Itzhak Perlman (b. 1945), made his television debut at the age of 14. He has performed with all the world's leading orchestras.

Moving the wrist back and forth evenly while pressing down on the strings makes the notes ring out – this is called *vibrato*

Violin

Plucked strings

THE HARP AND guitar have strings that are plucked to produce delicate, sweet music that is softer than most other instruments. The harp is often played in orchestras, but rarely has a leading role. The guitar is not an orchestral instrument, but it does feature in concertos.

The harp

The strings of the harp are set vibrating by the fingers, which sweep over them to produce beautiful cascades of notes. However, it is a difficult instrument to play. While plucking the 47 strings with the fingertips, the harpist also has to work seven foot pedals. The harp is used as an accompanying instrument, and is also performed solo.

PLAY TRACK 21

"Somber, plucked chords in the harp's middle and low registers give a melancholy, contemplative atmosphere to the seventh variation."

In the neck of the harp, each string passes over a pair of disks. The pedals operate the disks to change the pitch of the notes

The strings are made of gut, nylon, or steel. To help the harpist locate the right strings, each C string is colored red, and the F strings are black or purple. All the other strings are white

The right hand plucks the shorter strings, which produce higher notes, and the left hand plays the longer strings to give lower notes. Each hand can pluck up to four strings at once, enabling the harpist to play chords. The little fingers are never used

The harpist may stop the sounds of the strings by placing the palm of the hand on them to stop them from vibrating

The strings are fixed in the wooden soundboard. This is set vibrating by the strings, and amplifies the sound made by them

The wooden pillar contains rods that connect the pedals to the disks in the neck

Each of the seven pedals controls six or seven strings

Neck

World harpist
The Spanish musician, Marisa Robles (b. 1937), is famous worldwide for her brilliant harp playing. She is artistic director of the World Harp Festival, and has written harp pieces based on the *Narnia* books by C.S. Lewis.

Pedal power

Before playing, the harpist tunes the 47 strings of the harp to sequences of the notes A, B, C, D, E, F, and G – the same as the white keys of the piano. The seven pedals produce the other notes – the sharps and flats – which are like the black piano keys. The A pedal, for example, changes the pitch of all the A strings, making them either flat, natural, or sharp. The pedals work by changing the length of string that vibrates.

Flat notes
Each pedal has three notches. In the top notch, the pedal turns the pair of disks on each string connected to the pedal so that the disk pins do not touch the string. The string vibrates at its full length, giving a flat, or lower, note.

Natural notes
In the middle notch, the pedal turns the upper disk of the pair of disks on each of the connected strings. The pins on the upper disk grip the string so that the string vibrates at a shorter, or medium, length. This gives a natural, or normal, note.

Sharp notes
In the bottom notch, the pedal turns the lower disk of the pair of disks on each of the connected strings. The pins on the lower disk grip the string so that the vibrating length is at its shortest. This gives a sharp, or higher, note.

The guitar

The classical guitar originally came from Spain, and is therefore also known as the Spanish guitar. It is usually played solo, often in transcriptions of pieces for other instruments, and there are also concertos for guitar and orchestra. Many of the best guitar works are by Spanish composers.

The round hole in the soundboard helps it to vibrate

Neck

Tuning pegs

Bridge

Frets on the fingerboard enable the guitarist to press the strings at the correct positions

The six strings are made of nylon, or nylon wound with wire

The guitarist can use three fingers and thumb to play the strings, usually with the nails, or sweep the hand over the strings to strum the guitar and play chords

A footstool raises the guitar to a comfortable position for playing

Struts help transmit vibrations and also add strength

Top block joins neck of guitar to body

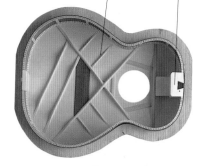

The soundboard
The most important part of the guitar is the top surface, or soundboard. It is set vibrating by the strings, and amplifies the sounds made by the strings so that the notes ring out loudly and clearly. Struts are glued inside the soundboard in a pattern that is crucial to the tone of the guitar.

The lute
The famous British guitarist, Julian Bream (b. 1933), also plays the lute. This is an early instrument with a curved back and up to 13 pairs of strings.

Woodwind instruments

N O FAMILY OF INSTRUMENTS has as much diversity of sound as the woodwinds. Eight of them can normally be heard in the orchestra, ranging from the shrill piccolo to the gruff tones of the contrabassoon. In between come the flute, the clarinet, the haunting bass clarinet, and the plaintive tones of the oboe, English horn, and bassoon. Unlike other instruments, the sound varies greatly depending on whether the instrument is at the top, middle, or bottom of its range, and composers exploit these sound contrasts in their music. There is chamber and solo music for woodwinds.

How woodwind instruments work

Blowing into the mouthpiece makes a column of air inside the tube of the instrument vibrate and produce sound. Changing the length of the air column makes the note lower or higher. Most woodwinds have reeds – a short length of cane in the mouthpiece that vibrates when a woodwind player blows into it.

The mouthpiece

A flautist blows across a hole in the mouthpiece. The edge of the hole breaks up the air stream, which sets the air inside the flute vibrating. In most other woodwinds, a reed in the mouthpiece makes the air vibrate.

Edge of hole

Air stream

Flute mouthpiece

Peak vibration of air

Mouthpiece

Covered holes

Long air column gives deep note

All holes covered

Zero vibration at center of air column

Peak vibration of air

Mouthpiece

Short air column gives high note

Three holes covered

Uncovered holes

The air column

The column of vibrating air extends from the mouthpiece to the first uncovered hole, or to the end of the tube if all holes are covered. Uncovering the holes shortens the air column and raises the pitch of the note. Covering the holes lengthens the air column and lowers the pitch.

The flute

Formerly wooden, most flutes are now made of metal – often silver, and sometimes even gold. They are made in three sections called joints, which can be moved in or out slightly to adjust the tuning. All the holes have pads that are closed directly by the fingers or by keys operated by the fingers. The low notes of the flute have a hollow sound, but in its upper range the tone is bright and brilliant.

PLAY TRACK 22

"Low flutes play soft, descending chords, their mellow sound reinforcing the melancholy tone created by the harp."

The holes on a flute are made wider than the fingers to give a good sound, so wide pads are used to close the holes instead of the fingers

The right thumb supports the weight of the flute, while the left thumb operates a pair of keys

Head joint

Body joint

Foot joint

The piccolo

Named after the Italian word for "little," the piccolo is a small flute. It has the same keywork as the flute, and many flautists also play the piccolo. It produces a high, shrill sound that can be clearly heard above the orchestra.

PLAY TRACK 32

"The high, piping piccolo brightens the sound and leads the other woodwinds and strings toward the end of the Finale."

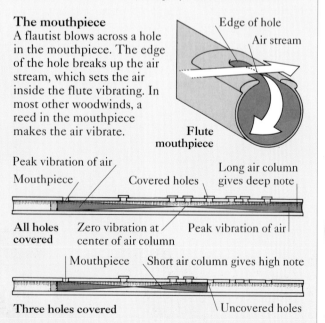

The piccolo is less than half the length of the flute. This one is made of black plastic with silver keys

The tube of the flute is stopped at the upper end

The flautist blows across a mouthpiece in the side of the tube.

The bass clarinet

Twice the length of the clarinet, the bass clarinet can produce deep notes with a dark, haunting tone. It has the same keywork as the clarinet, and many clarinetists also play the bass clarinet.

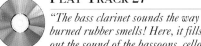

PLAY TRACK 27

"The bass clarinet sounds the way burned rubber smells! Here, it fills out the sound of the bassoons, cellos, and double basses as they all play the opening of the final fugue."

The upper part of the tube is curved downward to bring the mouthpiece within easy reach of the player's mouth

The clarinet

This is the B-flat clarinet, the standard kind of clarinet. Many clarinetists also play the A clarinet, which is slightly longer. Both kinds of clarinet have exactly the same keywork. Most clarinets are made of wood, and all have single reeds.

PLAY TRACK 21

"The clarinet plays in the low register, where its hollow, throaty sound blends with the low notes of the harp."

The metal bell curves upward to project the sound of the low notes forward

The cylindrical shape of the clarinet's tube gives it a smooth tone

A spike supports the weight of the instrument

The oboe

The tube of the oboe is conical, widening out into a bell at the end. This shape, together with the double reed in the mouthpiece, gives the oboe a plaintive tone. The oboe has holes that are closed directly by the fingers, or by pads and keys operated by the fingers.

PLAY TRACK 15

"The nasal tone of the oboes helps to recreate the sound of an orchestra in Purcell's time."

The oboist presses the lips together and turns them inward over the teeth

Flared bell

The body of the oboe is made of ebony or African blackwood

The English horn

Longer than the oboe, the English horn, or cor anglais, can produce deeper notes. It has the same arrangement of keys as the oboe, and many oboists also play the English horn. A neck cord takes the weight of the instrument.

PLAY TRACK 28

"The theme makes its second entry in the fugue on the English horn, blended with horns and viola – all instruments with warm, mellow sounds."

The reed, which is shorter than the oboe reed, fits into a curved metal crook, which is bent back to reach the player's mouth

Fingering is the same as for the oboe

The egg-shaped bell at the end of the tube gives the low notes a soft, velvety tone

Double reeds

The oboe, English horn, bassoon, and contrabassoon all have double reeds for mouthpieces. Many players make their own reeds. A strip of cane is bent in two, and the ends are bound together. The bend is sliced off to form a pair of reeds, which are then pared thin so that they vibrate easily. Before playing, the reeds are moistened. Then they are held between the lips and a stream of air is forced between them. This makes the two parts vibrate, producing a squawky sound.

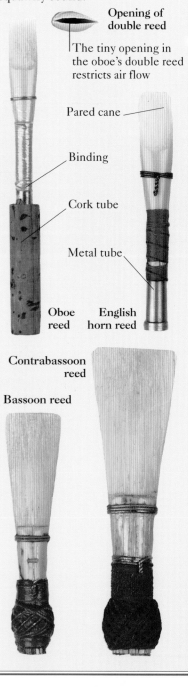

Opening of double reed

The tiny opening in the oboe's double reed restricts air flow

Pared cane

Binding

Cork tube

Metal tube

Oboe reed

English horn reed

Contrabassoon reed

Bassoon reed

The bassoon

Like the oboe, the bassoon has a double reed and a conical tube of wood, usually maple. The tube is four times as long as that of the oboe, and is folded in two so that the player can hold it easily – hence the Italian name for bassoon is *fagotto*, meaning "bundle of sticks." The bassoon works in the same way as the oboe, and has a similar plaintive, though deeper, sound.

Both thumbs operate keys, so a rest for the right hand helps to support the weight of the bassoon

PLAY TRACK 30

"As the oboes and clarinets continue the fugue, the deep, gobbling rhythm of the bassoons keeps up the momentum."

Decorative ivory ring

Slightly bulbous bell

Double reed fits into a curved crook

The tube of the bassoon is about 8 ft (2.5 m) long

Metal cap protects bend in tube

The contrabassoon

Really low notes come from the contrabassoon, or double bassoon, which is like a bassoon but has a tube twice as long. It is usually folded into four, and a metal peg supports the weight of the instrument. The keywork is the same as for the bassoon, so a bassoonist can also play the contrabassoon.

PLAY TRACK 29

"Deep beneath the orchestra, the contrabassoon plays a long, low note – like a gentle snore."

A metal bell helps to project the low notes of the contra-bassoon

Woodwind playing

WITH JUST EIGHT FINGERS and two thumbs, a woodwind player can produce up to 40 different notes on an instrument. This is because the little fingers each press several keys. Also, operating just one thumb key or simply blowing harder can change the range and cause the same finger combinations to give higher notes. Controlled, even blowing is essential to a good sound on all woodwind instruments.

Cane reed

Ligature secures reed

Single reeds
The clarinet mouthpiece is a hollow chamber with an opening on the underside, over which a single reed fits. The reed is held in place by a screw clamp called a ligature. The mouthpiece fits into the top of the clarinet tube. Blowing into it makes the tip of the reed vibrate, which sets the air vibrating inside the tube to produce a sound.

While blowing, the player often begins a note or phrase by quickly drawing back the tongue. This makes the sound start cleanly

The cylindrical bore gives the clarinet its characteristic smooth tone

The position and shape of the lips are called the embouchure

The player blows evenly without puffing out the cheeks

The left thumb closes a hole and operates a key at the back of the tube that controls the register, causing a note to sound in either the high or low range of the instrument

Parts of the instrument

Woodwind instruments can be dismantled so that they can be cleaned easily after playing and packed into a carrying case for protection. The sections, or joints, have to fit tightly together because a leak would give a wrong note or unpleasant sound.

Mouthpiece

Barrel joint can be moved in or out to tune the instrument

Keys for left little finger

Bell

Upper joint with keys for left hand

Lower joint with keys for right hand

Greased cork ring to seal joints

The keywork

The fingers may open and close a hole directly, but many holes are out of reach of the fingers, and some instruments have large holes that are too big for the fingers to cover. These holes have pads that are closed by keys or rings, which in turn are operated by the fingers. A spring raises the pad to open the hole when a key or ring is released.

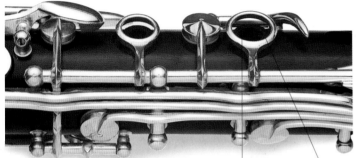

Clarinet's uncovered holes   Hole   Ring

Oboe's covered holes   Rod connecting key to pad   Key   Pad

Nonorchestral woodwinds

Two popular instruments that belong to the woodwind family are the saxophone and the recorder. Neither are played much in orchestras, but the saxophone is often heard in jazz, while the recorder is a simple instrument that is good for beginners and for playing early music.

The saxophone

Made of metal, the saxophone has a conical tube and keywork like the oboe, and a single reed mouthpiece like the clarinet. It can sound sweet or harsh, depending on how it is blown.

PLAY TRACK 11

"The saxophone is used for its jazz associations – here it plays a blueslike variation on Purcell's original theme."

The recorder

Like the flute, the recorder mouthpiece has no reed. Made of wood or plastic, soprano and alto recorders have no keys, while tenor and bass recorders have just one key.

Soprano recorder

The lowest holes are covered by pads operated by keys under the little fingers of both hands

The little finger of the right hand operates four keys

The clarinet tube is usually made of African blackwood

The end of the tube widens out into a bell that helps to project the low notes outward

Young winner
The British clarinetist, Emma Johnson (b. 1966) came to fame in 1984 by winning a nationwide television contest for the best young musician of the year. She is now one of the most famous clarinetists in the world, performing throughout Europe, Japan, and America.

Clarinet

Brass instruments

THRILLING FANFARES and blazing climaxes are the kind of music at which brass excels. Gleaming in gold and silver, the orchestra's brass section both looks and sounds majestic. The trumpet makes the highest notes, the horn and trombone sound the middle range, and at the bottom is the tuba, its deep boom underpinning the rest of the brass. There is some chamber and solo music for brass instruments.

How brass instruments work

A brass instrument is a long metal tube that is bent into coils to make it easier to hold. Blowing into a mouthpiece at one end of the tube causes the air inside to vibrate and produce a sound.

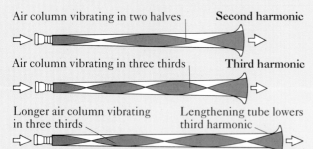

Air column vibrating in two halves — Second harmonic

Air column vibrating in three thirds — Third harmonic

Longer air column vibrating in three thirds — Lengthening tube lowers third harmonic

Lowered third harmonic

Getting the notes

By tightening the lips more and more, a brass player can make an air column vibrate in halves, thirds, and so on. This gives a set of notes called harmonics. The notes between the harmonics are produced by lengthening the tube, which lowers the pitch of each harmonic.

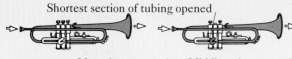

Shortest section of tubing opened

Valves

No valves pressed — Middle valve pressed

Most brass instruments have three valves that open side sections of tubing to increase the length of the whole tube. Pressing the valves in six different combinations lengthens the tube by different amounts to give the six notes beneath each harmonic.

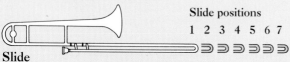

Slide positions
1 2 3 4 5 6 7

Slide

The trombone has a sliding section of tubing that can be moved out to lengthen the tube. Six positions (numbered 2 to 7) give the six notes beneath each harmonic produced at the first position.

The trumpet

This is the B-flat trumpet, the standard orchestral model. Some trumpet players also play the piccolo trumpet, a smaller version that produces very high notes, and the cornet, which is the same size as the trumpet but has a fatter, less piercing sound.

PLAY TRACK 24

"The trumpet is muted, which gives the notes an icy quality; here and there the player bends a note."

The cylindrical bore gives the trumpet its bright tone

The very wide bell helps to make the sound rich and resonant

The valves are operated by the right hand

The long tube gives the tuba its deep notes

The tuba

There are several different sizes of tuba, each with a different range of notes. The tube is conical and widens out dramatically to give a warmer sound than the trombone. The tuba can be played more softly and nimbly than its great size suggests.

PLAY TRACK 13

"The tuba has a comical image, but its beautifully smooth tone enables it to carry this somber melody."

The weight of the tuba rests on the legs

The trombone

This is a tenor, or standard, trombone. Its tube is twice as long as the trumpet's, and has the same narrow cylindrical bore that produces a bright sound. Some players prefer the bass trombone, which has an extra length of tubing to give lower notes.

The horn

Also known as the French horn, this instrument is actually two horns in one. Between the mouthpiece and bell, the tube divides into two long coiled tubes of different length. The player switches from one to the other by pressing a fourth valve with the left thumb, so extending the range of the horn without sacrificing tone quality.

PLAY TRACK 31

"Purcell's witches' theme reappears, rising majestically with the strident sound of the trombones."

The trombonist can move the slide slowly so that one note glides into the next

Water key

Slide brace held by right hand

Because it is so big and full of air, it takes a great deal of breath to play the tuba

PLAY TRACK 7

"Behind the soft strings, the horn players blow two long notes, bending each one by pushing the hand slowly across and into the bell— the effect is eerie."

The funnel-shaped mouthpiece and long, narrow conical tube give the horn a more mellow tone than the trumpet

Lever

The fingers of the left hand press three levers that work the valves

Rotary valve opens side section of tubing

The right hand may be inserted into the bell to soften the sound

Brass playing

BLOWING A BRASS instrument requires a lot of effort and even some strain, especially when playing high or loud. Good control of the lips is needed to reach the higher notes, as well as to produce a good tone. It's quite easy to strive for a particular harmonic and miss it or "crack" a note. Constant practice helps to strengthen the lip muscles. Brass players also need to do regular breathing exercises to develop the diaphragm.

Cups and funnels

Brass instruments have mouthpieces with cup- or funnel-shaped openings. A cup-shape makes a brighter sound than a funnel-shape. Inside is a small tube that fits into the body of the instrument. The lips are pressed together against the mouthpiece and air is blown through them. This makes the lips vibrate and produce a sound.

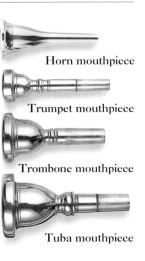

Horn mouthpiece

Trumpet mouthpiece

Trombone mouthpiece

Tuba mouthpiece

Most brass instruments are made of brass that has been lacquered or plated to make cleaning easier. This trumpet is gold-lacquered

The narrow metal tube has a cylinder-shaped bore

Three fingertips of the right hand operate the valve pistons

Finger button

Finger rest

The lips are pressed against the mouthpiece

This side section of tubing is opened by the first valve

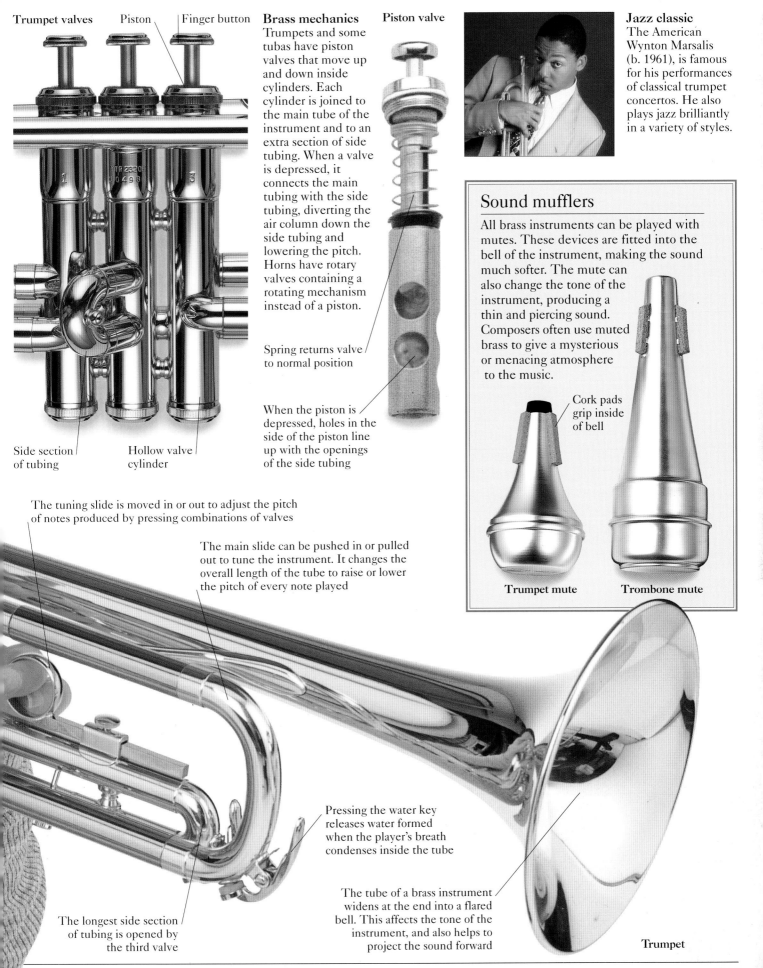

Trumpet valves   Piston   Finger button

1   3

Side section
of tubing

Hollow valve
cylinder

Brass mechanics

Trumpets and some tubas have piston valves that move up and down inside cylinders. Each cylinder is joined to the main tube of the instrument and to an extra section of side tubing. When a valve is depressed, it connects the main tubing with the side tubing, diverting the air column down the side tubing and lowering the pitch. Horns have rotary valves containing a rotating mechanism instead of a piston.

Spring returns valve
to normal position

When the piston is depressed, holes in the side of the piston line up with the openings of the side tubing

Piston valve

Jazz classic

The American Wynton Marsalis (b. 1961), is famous for his performances of classical trumpet concertos. He also plays jazz brilliantly in a variety of styles.

Sound mufflers

All brass instruments can be played with mutes. These devices are fitted into the bell of the instrument, making the sound much softer. The mute can also change the tone of the instrument, producing a thin and piercing sound. Composers often use muted brass to give a mysterious or menacing atmosphere to the music.

Cork pads
grip inside
of bell

Trumpet mute   **Trombone mute**

The tuning slide is moved in or out to adjust the pitch of notes produced by pressing combinations of valves

The main slide can be pushed in or pulled out to tune the instrument. It changes the overall length of the tube to raise or lower the pitch of every note played

Pressing the water key releases water formed when the player's breath condenses inside the tube

The longest side section of tubing is opened by the third valve

The tube of a brass instrument widens at the end into a flared bell. This affects the tone of the instrument, and also helps to project the sound forward

Trumpet

Percussion instruments

A LOUD BANG on the drum, or a crash of cymbals, often helps to bring music to an exciting climax. The tambourine can play energetic rhythms that drive the music along or make it dance. These "unpitched" percussion instruments make sounds that do not have a particular pitch. But there are also "pitched," or tuned percussion instruments that produce notes with a definite pitch. Percussionists in orchestras can play the whole range of percussion instruments – unpitched and tuned – and often walk from one to another during a performance. Percussion instruments are almost always played in orchestras and bands; there is little chamber or solo music written for them.

How percussion instruments work

A percussionist strikes a percussion instrument with a stick or mallet, or sometimes a hand, to produce a sound. When a cymbal or gong is struck, the whole instrument vibrates. When a xylophone is played, only the bars that are struck vibrate to produce sound. When a drum is played, the skin vibrates, and the air inside the drum vibrates too, making the sound louder.

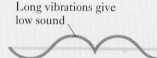

Short vibrations give high sound

Small drum skin

Long vibrations give low sound

Large drum skin

Good vibrations

Hitting the stretched skin of a drum makes it vibrate. As the sound rings out, the skin moves rapidly up and down like waves rippling across the surface of water. A small drum produces a higher sound than a large drum because the width of the vibrating skin is smaller. The metal discs of gongs and cymbals also vibrate in this way.

Unpitched percussion

Stringed, woodwind, brass, and keyboard instruments all make notes with a definite pitch because they contain strings or air columns that vibrate at definite rates. Unpitched percussion instruments, such as cymbals, some gongs, and most drums, do not vibrate at a particular rate, causing them to emit an unpitched sound rather than a pitched note.

Leather strap

Cymbals

A pair of thin metal discs, the cymbals are held by leather straps attached at the center of each cymbal. When they are clashed together, the percussionist has to take care not to trap air between them, as this muffles the sound.

Timpani

The most common percussion instruments in an orchestra are the timpani, also called kettledrums. They vary in width, and the skin, or head, of each drum is tightened to produce a pitched note. The timpanist tunes the drums to give a particular set of notes, and often plays a passage on several timpani.

Damping
The timpanist can stop the note from echoing, by pressing a hand or fingers against the skin.

The timpanist plays the skin of the drum near the rim

PLAY TRACK 3

"The timpani beat away beneath the orchestra, bringing the first variation to a grand climax with a roll on the last chord."

The tuning gauge indicates the pitch of the note produced by pressing the pedal

The skin, or head, of the drum is made of plastic or calf skin

The shell, or round bowl, is usually made of copper

Operating the pedal tightens or loosens the skin, which changes the note of the drum

Roto-toms

Unlike unpitched orchestral drums such as the large bass drum, which gives a deep resounding boom, and the side, or snare, drum which produces a higher, crisp sound, roto-toms are drums that can be tuned. Rotating the drum on its stand or pressing a pedal tightens or loosens the skin, which changes the pitch of the note. Roto-toms have a clear, resonant sound, and are made in a range of sizes – the smaller ones give higher notes. They are often used in schools instead of timpani because they are less expensive.

Tam-tam

Gongs are often used to give a piece of music an atmosphere of mystery or menace. The tam-tam is a type of gong that gives a deep, ringing sound with no definite pitch. When struck strongly, it erupts with a violent and thunderous burst of noise. There are also tuned gongs that produce particular notes.

PLAY TRACK 9

"The ominous ring of the tam-tam behind the strings gives dramatic impact to the eerie opening of the fourth variation."

Left hand placed behind gong to dampen sound

Small roto-toms do not have pedals; turning the frame changes the note over a range of about an octave

A roto-tom consists only of a stretched skin in a circular frame. It has no cylindrical shell

A large beater is used to strike the tam-tam

The sound rings for a long time as the disk continues to vibrate

The struts contain the mechanism that alters the note

Pressing the pedal alters the pitch of the note being played

The bronze disk of the tam-tam is suspended from a frame

Tuned percussion

Some percussion instruments have rows of bars, or tubes, usually made of metal; each bar gives a definite note when struck, and vibrates to sound at a pitch that depends on its length – the longer the bar, the deeper the note. The bars or tubes are arranged in two rows in the same way as the black and white keys on a piano keyboard, with sharps or flats behind the natural notes.

The percussionist strikes the tube at a point near the top with a mallet

Tubular bells

The sound of bells ringing out from an orchestra comes from a set of long brass or steel tubes hanging in a frame. The percussionist strikes the tubes with mallets, causing them to ring out with a sound similar to that of church bells. A set of tubular bells contains up to 25 tubes.

PLAY TRACK 23

"Like a church bell, a tubular bell twice signals the entry of a solemn phrase on deep trumpets."

Glockenspiel

The orchestral glockenspiel contains a set of up to 42 steel bars arranged like the keys on a piano keyboard. The percussionist strikes the bars using two hardheaded beaters to produce bright, penetrating bell sounds. Marching bands use portable glockenspiels held in one hand and played with the other.

PLAY TRACK 3

"The bell-like tones of the glockenspiel ring out high above the orchestra."

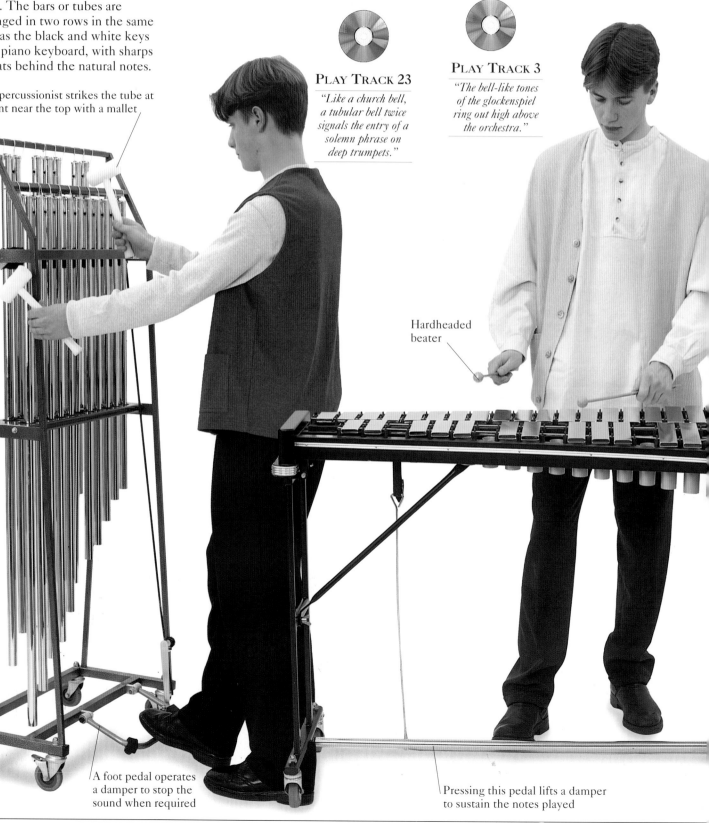

Hardheaded beater

A foot pedal operates a damper to stop the sound when required

Pressing this pedal lifts a damper to sustain the notes played

Vibraphone

The orchestra's tuned percussion instruments – the xylophone and the vibraphone – have vertical tubes, called resonators, beneath a set of bars. When hit with a mallet, a bar vibrates and sets the air inside the tube vibrating too, making the sound louder. The xylophone, which has wooden bars, produces a dry, brittle sound, but the vibraphone gives a mellow, sweet tone. It is called a vibraphone because the sound can be made to vibrate, or throb, by means of an electric motor – this effect can be switched off.

PLAY TRACK 23

"The high, glassy notes of the vibraphone blend with the celesta to give an angelic sound that makes a perfect accompaniment to the harp."

Principal percussionist
The British virtuoso Evelyn Glennie (b. 1965) is famous for her solo percussion performances and for playing works that feature percussion, some commissioned for her by leading composers.

A vibraphone player can stop a note from sounding by gently touching the bar with a beater

A player can use four beaters to play chords

MUSSER

At the top of each resonating tube is a rotating disk turned by an electric motor. This gives the vibraphone its throbbing sound

Some glockenspiels have resonating tubes for the lower notes

Pressing the damper pedal sustains all the notes being played; it works in the same way as the sustaining pedal on a piano

Resonator

Beating a rhythm

Percussionists use a variety of implements, generally called beaters, to play their instruments. Side drums require wooden sticks. Timpani and tuned percussion are played with sticks or beaters with different types of head – some soft and others hard – to produce different sounds.

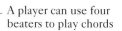

Timpani stick

Tubular bell mallet

Roto-tom stick

Glockenspiel beater

Tam-tam beater

Vibraphone beater

Keyboard instruments

NO OTHER GROUP of instruments makes such complete music as the keyboards. Because all the fingers and thumbs can each play a note, a keyboard instrument can produce a vast range of music – massive chords, rapid runs of notes, a tune with an accompaniment, or several melodies at once. Keyboard instruments include the piano, harpsichord, organ, and synthesizer. They all have the same arrangement of keys, so a keyboard player can switch from one to another quite easily.

How a piano works

Inside a piano is a set of stretched wires, called strings. A series of levers links each key to a felt-tipped hammer, which rises and strikes a string when the key is pressed. This mechanism is very responsive to the pianist's touch, and enables the pianist to play softly and loudly. Pianoforte, the piano's full name, means "soft-loud" in Italian.

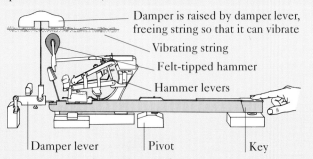

Damper is raised by damper lever, freeing string so that it can vibrate

Vibrating string

Felt-tipped hammer

Hammer levers

Damper lever   Pivot   Key

Pressing a key
As a key is pressed, the far end tilts up, causing the levers to push up the hammer and raise the damper. The hammer hits the string, which vibrates and produces a note.

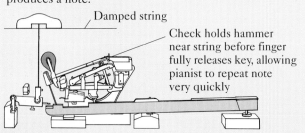

Damped string

Check holds hammer near string before finger fully releases key, allowing pianist to repeat note very quickly

Releasing the key
As the key is released, the far end falls back, and the levers lower the hammer and damper. The sound of the note fades away as the damper touches the string and stops it from vibrating.

The grand piano

Professional pianists play the grand piano – a large piano with a horizontal body. An upright piano, by contrast, has a vertical body and therefore occupies less space. Both instruments work in the same way, but the grand piano has a richer tone. The grand piano is the solo instrument in piano concertos, and composers such as Stravinsky, Copland, and Bartók include a piano as part of the orchestra. There is much chamber music and a wealth of solo music for the piano.

PLAY TRACK 18
"A frantic, aggressive torrent of rising note clusters bursts forth from the piano as it introduces the battery of percussion instruments."

The seat of the piano stool can be raised or lowered to give a comfortable sitting position

Opening the lid increases the sound volume

The pianist's fingers are curved to play the keys with the fingertips. In this position, the fingers can exert their maximum control and strength

Inside the piano

The wire strings inside the piano are stretched on an iron frame and pass over a wooden bridge. The bridge transmits the vibrations of the strings to the soundboard, a flat piece of wood beneath the strings that amplifies the sound. The lowest bass strings are thick single strings. The higher tenor strings are double strings (pairs of strings), and the remaining treble strings are triple strings (sets of three strings).

Soundboard

Bass strings give low notes

The bass and tenor strings cross over the treble strings to make them longer

Treble strings give high notes

Tenor strings give middle-range notes

Bridge

Dampers stop strings from vibrating

Hammers strike strings, making them vibrate

Tuning pins adjust the tension of the strings

The sustaining pedal lifts the dampers off all the strings so that they continue to sound when the keys are released, making the notes last a long time

The soft pedal moves the keyboard and hammers sideways, so that only one string of each note is struck. This makes the notes sound softer and sweeter

Dedicated to Mozart
The Japanese pianist Mitsuko Uchida (b. 1948) has given piano recitals and performed piano concertos with major orchestras throughout the world. She is particularly renowned for the beauty and clarity of her playing of Mozart's piano music.

The celesta

The delicate, high chimes of the celesta can sometimes be heard ringing out in orchestral pieces. This keyboard instrument, which resembles a small upright piano, is only played as part of the orchestra, and never on its own. It occasionally has a principal role, as in the famous *Dance of the Sugarplum Fairy* from *The Nutcracker Suite* by Peter Tchaikovsky, but composers tend to use the celesta for decorative effects. The instrument was invented by Auguste Mustel in France in 1886.

PLAY TRACK 22

"The tinkling tones of the celesta blend with the vibraphone to give an angelic sound that makes a perfect accompaniment to the harp."

49-note keyboard (some instruments have 61 notes)

Pedal sustains notes by lifting dampers from the bars

Sound escapes through slots in the front and sides of the celesta

How it works

Each key of the celesta is attached to a felt-tipped hammer, as in the piano. But instead of striking strings, the hammers hit steel bars of different lengths, which ring out with a bell-like tone. Each bar rests on a hollow wooden box that resonates and gives the sound an ethereal quality.

Steel bars

Pedal operates dampers

Inside the celesta

The harpsichord

The music of a harpsichord comes from one or more sets of wire strings, like those on a piano. But harpsichord strings are plucked, not struck like the strings on a piano, and this gives a bright, silvery sound that does not vary in volume. The harpsichord is mainly heard in music composed before about 1750. It features in concertos and is also played as part of the orchestra. There is much chamber and solo music for the harpsichord.

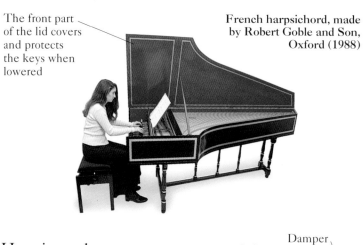

The front part of the lid covers and protects the keys when lowered

French harpsichord, made by Robert Goble and Son, Oxford (1988)

How it works

Each key of a harpsichord moves a plectrum, which plucks a string when the key is pressed. The key tilts on a balance point, and connects to a jack containing a plectrum made of quill, leather, or plastic. The plectrum normally rests under the string. At the top of the jack is a damper, which rests on top of the string.

Pressing a key
The far end of the key pushes up the jack, causing the plectrum to pluck the string. As the jack rises, the damper lifts off the string, leaving it free to vibrate and produce a sound.

Releasing the key
The jack descends, and the tongue carrying the plectrum tilts back so that the plectrum passes the string without plucking it again. The damper comes to rest on the string, stopping it from vibrating so that the note dies away.

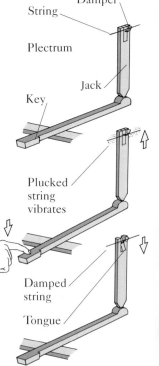

Damper

String

Plectrum

Jack

Key

Plucked string vibrates

Damped string

Tongue

Harpsichord talent
The British musician, Virginia Black (b. 1950) is famous for her playing of harpsichord music by J.S. Bach and Domenico Scarlatti. She has toured in the US, Europe, Australia, and New Zealand, and is professor of harpsichord at the Royal Academy of Music in London.

Pulling out the stops

A harpsichordist can use stops that make the strings produce different sounds. Some stops couple strings together so that each key makes a pair of strings vibrate and give a bigger sound. Other stops produce a softer tone by muting the strings.

This brass lever engages a set of strings that can be played from the lower manual (keyboard)

This knob links both manuals so that they can play at the same time

Transposing device

Close-up of harpsichord keyboard

The nameboard has details of the maker, and year and place of manufacture of the harpsichord

This harpsichord has a second manual, with extra strings that give it a different tone from the first manual

ROBERT GOBLE & SON + C

Like many harpsichords, this instrument has black natural keys and white sharp and flat keys

The strings are laid over bridges attached to the soundboard, which resonates and enriches the sound

Behind the music stand is the buff stop, which moves a series of leather pads against the strings to mute them

The organ

Hundreds of pipes, ranked in rows above and around a
set of manuals (keyboards), make the pipe organ the
largest musical instrument of all. The organist selects
different ranks (rows) of pipes to vary the sound of the
organ, which can range from a mighty roar down to the
merest whisper of sound. Most concert halls and
churches have an organ. With its great variety of sound,
the organ is principally a solo instrument, but it is
sometimes played with the orchestra, as in Camille
Saint-Saëns' Third Symphony.

Leading organist
The British musician
Peter Hurford (b. 1930)
is one of the world's
leading organists.
He is famous for his
recording of the
complete organ works
of J.S. Bach, and has
made concert tours of
Europe, America,
Japan, and Australasia.

How it works

Electricity powers this organ. When it is switched on, a fan starts to spin,
creating wind. The wind travels via channels into wind chests, on which the
pipes rest. When a key is pressed, it opens a valve in the wind chest, letting
air into a pipe. Pulling out a stop links the keys of a manual to a particular
set of pipes with a certain sound. Some stops give the familiar organ sound,
while other pipes imitate instruments such as flutes, trumpets, and strings.

Console
The set of manuals, stops, and pedals at which an organist sits is called
the console. A pipe organ has between one and five manuals – this one
has four, called (from top to bottom) Solo, Swell, Great, and Choir. Each
manual has 61 keys (some instruments have 56), but its full range of
notes is much greater as the stops can
bring in high- or low-sounding pipes.

The Swell
manual's pipes
are enclosed in
a swell box with
shutters which
can be opened to
"swell" the sound

The Great
manual is
connected to
these stops

These stops
are linked
to the Solo
manual

The Solo manual's
stops have sounds for
playing melodies. Its
pipes are enclosed in
a swell box

The Choir
manual
works with
these stops

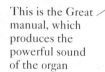

This is the Great
manual, which
produces the
powerful sound
of the organ

The Choir manual
produces a soft,
delicate sound

Toe pistons operate
pedal stops

These two big
pedals open and
close the shutters
of the swell boxes

This piston cancels
all stops pulled out

To make it easier
to operate stops
while playing, the
organist can press
thumb pistons,
which work the
stops automatically

Both feet are used to
press these 32 large
keys, which are laid
out like the black
and white keys of a
piano keyboard

| The organ | Mouth of pipe | Organ gallery | Choir pipes | Console | Great pipes are connected to the great manual | Trackers join console to pipes | Pedal towers contain the largest, lowest pipes, which are played by the pedal keys | Channels leading from wind chest |

The synthesizer

A near-perfect imitator of all other instruments, the synthesizer can also produce natural sounds, voices, sound effects, and entirely new sounds never heard before. The keys vary the pitch of the sound, as in other keyboard instruments. The controls can select a particular sound at the press of a button – it comes from a "bank" of sounds stored in electronic form in the synthesizer's memory. When it is played, the synthesizer produces an electric signal that goes to an amplifier and loudspeaker, which gives out the sound. Some new music uses a synthesizer as part of the orchestra.

PLAY TRACK 10

"A run of rising notes from the synthesizer introduces the saxophone melody. The programed sound is a blend of vibraphone and hand bells that bend as the sound dies away."

Controls can be used to create and store new sounds

Synthesizer player

Synthesizer keyboard

Chamber music

MUSIC THAT IS suitable for performance in a chamber or room is called chamber music. In the past, it was performed in the private halls of royalty and the aristocracy, but today professional musicians play chamber music in concert halls. Chamber groups contain from three up to about eight players – pieces for one or two players are not considered to be chamber music. A piece of chamber music is like a musical discussion, in which the performers continually answer each other's statements. Each player contributes equally, and all the instruments play most of the time. Individual musicians have the opportunity to use their personal interpretation of the music. In orchestral music, by contrast, players can have long pauses where they do not play, and all must conform to a general spirit of interpretation.

Early quartet
Composers in Italy, Germany, and Austria pioneered the string quartet from about 1750 onward. In many early quartets, there was less interplay between the instruments and the four players did not need to look at each other while playing.

The string quartet

Two violins, a viola, and a cello make up a string quartet. This combination of instruments from the string family blends to give a full, rich sound when all play together; the four instruments can each play individual melodies, or combine in various subgroups to accompany one another. Composers such as Joseph Haydn, Ludwig van Beethoven, and Béla Bartok have made use of the wide range of musical expression available to the string quartet to write some of their most lyrical and intense music.

The leader starts the music with a signal of the bow

First violin
As leader of the quartet, the first violin sits on the left. Because it plays in a higher register than the viola and cello, the violin usually has a leading role, and often plays the main tune.

Second violin
The accompaniment to the first violin is usually led by the second violin, but often both violins lead the music together, playfully exchanging fragments of the main tune.

Modern quartet

The Kronos Quartet, an American string quartet, was founded 21 years ago. Professional quartets tend to remain together for many years, during which time they develop the great sensitivity necessary to perform this form of chamber music. The Kronos Quartet specializes in new music, while most other string quartets devote themselves mainly to the great quartets of the past.

Viola

Beneath the high violins and above the low cello, the viola occupies the middle range of the string quartet. It provides an inner texture, its warm tone filling out the music.

Eye contact between players is important when playing in a string quartet

Cello

The lowest line of music is usually played by the cello, which provides a foundation for the violins and viola. The cello may also play a singing melody beneath an accompaniment by the other three strings.

The players sit in a wide semicircle so that they can all see each other easily

The wind quintet

The instruments that make up a wind quintet are the flute, oboe, clarinet, bassoon, and horn. These five wind instruments make very different sounds, unlike the instruments in a string quartet, which sound similar. The wind quintet has more musical variety than most other chamber groups. It is easy to hear the individual instruments, and to appreciate how the different parts fit together to create the music. Most wind quintet music dates from the 20th century. One of the best examples is a wind quintet written in 1922 by Carl Nielsen, a Danish composer.

Flute

The highest instrument in the quintet is the flute, which may lead the music and ring out clearly above the other high woodwinds. It is also the most agile of the five instruments, and is ideal for decorative effects, such as fast runs and trills.

Oboe

Being in the same high range as the clarinet and flute, the oboe may play the main tune with them, or all three instruments may toss fragments of melody between one another.

Some wind quintets use an English horn instead of the oboe

Its plaintive tone enables the oboe to cut through and be heard among the other quintet sounds

Music stands are fixed quite low, so the players can see each other easily above their music

---

Chamber music groups

Chamber groups and the music written for them are named after the number of players involved, as in Haydn's String Quartet in C ("*Emperor*"), written for four players. The piano is used in some chamber group combinations.

Trios – 3 players

String trio
Violin, viola, cello
•Mozart Divertimento in E-flat major (K.563)

Piano trio
Piano, violin, cello
•Haydn Piano Trio no. 1 in G major

Quartets – 4 players

String quartet
2 violins, viola, cello
•Borodin String Quartet no. 2 in D major

Piano quartet
Piano, violin, viola, cello
•Schumann Piano Quartet in E-flat major

Quintets – 5 players

String quintet
2 violins, 2 violas, cello
•Beethoven String Quintet in C major

OR
2 violins, viola, 2 cellos
•Schubert String Quintet in C major

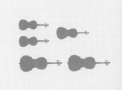

Bassoon
The deepest notes come from the bassoon, giving a solid foundation to the music. This instrument can also play rhythmic patterns that drive the music along, while its gruff sounds often lend humor to the music.

Clarinet
The lower notes of the clarinet take it below the flute and oboe into the middle range of the quintet, where its warm tone may fill out the music. In its high range, the clarinet is the strongest instrument, and may dominate the other high woodwinds.

Horn
Because it can play louder than the other instruments, the horn is often given strong melodies. Its powerful sound can be used for dramatic effect at the climax of a piece, or to add a sense of grandeur to the music.

Its distinctly reedy sound makes the clarinet stand out in solo passages

The horn may occupy the central position instead of the bassoon

When muted, the horn produces a piercing sound very different from the other instruments

When all the instruments play together, the blend of sound is rich and harmonious, while solo passages allow each instrument to show its distinctive character

Piano quintet
Piano, 2 violins, viola, cello
•Dvořák Piano Quintet in A major

OR

Piano, violin, viola, cello, double bass
•Schubert Piano Quintet in A major ("*The Trout*")

Clarinet quintet
Clarinet, 2 violins, viola, cello
•Mozart Clarinet Quintet in A major

Sextets – 6 players

String sextet
2 violins, 2 violas, 2 cellos
•Brahms Sextet no. 1 in B-flat major and Sextet no. 2 in G major

Octets – 8 players

String octet
4 violins, 2 violas, 2 cellos
•Mendelssohn Octet in E-flat major

Wind octet
2 oboes, 2 clarinets, 2 bassoons, 2 horns
•Mozart Serenade in E-flat major (K.375)

Ancient Minoan
harpist

Medieval viola
player

Baroque horn
player

Classical
cellist

Romantic lyre
player

PART TWO

THE HISTORY OF MUSIC

MUSIC HAS BEEN played and written for thousands of years. There is so much music to play, and so many works have been recorded, that it can be difficult to remember who wrote which piece. Some background information about the history of music and the achievements of the major composers can help.

This section of the book begins with a timeline, which describes the main milestones in the history of music from the earliest times through to the present day. It charts the great innovations, such as when people first began to write music down and when they started to compose music in more than one part. It indicates when the major musical forms, such as the concerto and the string quartet, were first written. And it singles out some of the most important and influential pieces of music from each historical period. All

this information helps to put music in its historical context, and shows how music changed from one period to the next.

The timeline is followed by an A–Z of composers. This contains short accounts of some 70 major composers, giving their dates and nationalities, describing briefly their contribution to the history of music, and listing some of their major works. Finally, a short section on musical forms defines some of the most popular types of music, such as the sonata and the symphony.

Ravel, a composer
of national music

Guitarist of
revolutionary era

Modern bass player

An ancient priest
blows the shofar, a
type of horn used on
solemn occasions in
Jewish synagogues.
The instrument's
sinuous curving
design is based
on a ram's horn

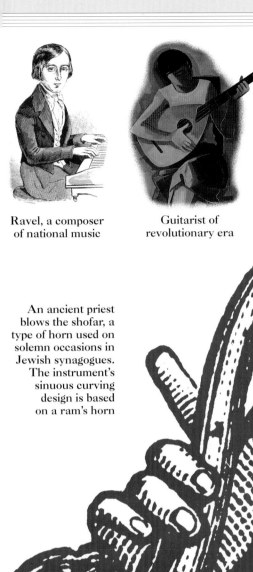

Up to AD 999
Ancient music

THE FIRST MUSIC was probably made by prehistoric people calling to each other or chanting. Simple instruments some 40,000 years old have been found, but music with definite melodies and rhythms using more elaborate instruments was first produced about 5,000 years ago, with the rise of the civilizations of Egypt and western Asia. These people used music in religious ceremonies and at important state occasions, but in ancient Greece, music became popular as an everyday activity. With the rise of Christianity about 1,500 years ago, monasteries became the main musical centers. Monks used plainsong, single-line music chanted to freely flowing melodies. The simple plainsong melodies developed into more complex forms, and this became the basis of the classical music that we enjoy today.

40,000 BC

People in France make whistles from reindeer toe bones. These produce only one note, and are probably used for signaling rather than for music. People also blow hollow horns and shells to make notes for signaling. Other prehistoric instruments, possibly made for music, include flutes made from hollow bones drilled with holes and bones carved with notches to make scrapers.

Reindeer bone whistles, c.40,000 BC

2600

An 11-string harp is made for Puabi, queen of the city of Ur, Mesopotamia (modern Iraq). Decorated with a bull's head, this instrument was discovered in the Royal Tombs of Ur and has been reconstructed by archaeologists. Apart from items such as bones and shells, it is the earliest musical instrument to have survived to the present day.

2000

In the rituals performed in the great temples of the Mesopotamian cities, simple chants develop into more elaborate pieces. In a new style of performance, priests and choirs sing alternate passages of the music. Reed pipes, flutes, drums, and tambourines are used for the accompaniment. These instruments may be played by the singers while they are singing.

220

Ctesibius of Alexandria (flourished c.246–221 BC) invents the hydraulis, a water-powered organ. It contains a set of pipes mounted on a chest, into which air is forced by water pressure. To open and close the pipes, the organist pushes sliders containing holes into and out of the chest.

500-400

The Greek philosopher Pythagoras (c.582–c.497 BC) employs mathematics to define the pitches of the scales of notes used in western music ever since. The Greeks then begin to write music, using letters of the alphabet for different pitches.

600

Orchestras play music for state events in Assyria. A victory of the Assyrian king Ashurbanipal (668–626 BC) is celebrated by an orchestra with harps, double-reed pipes, a drum, and a choir of 15 women.

AD 284

The ancient Romans use music to form part of big public events, such as the games and combats in the Colosseum, Rome. A huge concert is held at the games in Rome, featuring 100 trumpets, 100 horns, and 200 pipes. The Christians reject such vulgarity, and link instrumental music with paganism.

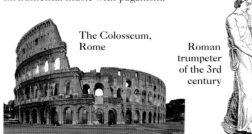

The Colosseum, Rome

Roman trumpeter of the 3rd century

300

Chinese music, until now cut off from contact with the rest of the world, comes under the influence of Buddhist music from central Asia. Popular instruments include the lute, seven-string zither, and various forms of pipes.

Ancient Chinese terra-cotta figure of a piper

300-400

Christianity becomes an authorized religion in the Roman Empire. With the fall of Rome in 410 and the split of the empire into eastern and western empires, two separate traditions evolve. In the western empire, based in Rome, western Christian music starts to develop. In the eastern empire, with its capital at Constantinople (modern Istanbul), priests keep to the old religious rites.
The music of the Roman church will become the basis of western classical music.

Sant' Eustachio, one of the earliest Christian churches in the city of Rome

THE CHANGING WORLD

The step pyramid at Saqqara

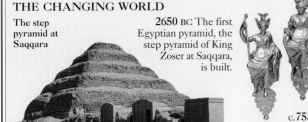

2650 BC The first Egyptian pyramid, the step pyramid of King Zoser at Saqqara, is built.

c.461 BC Democracy flourishes in Athens under the statesman Pericles.
332 BC Macedonian emperor Alexander the Great conquers Egypt.
c.265 BC The Mauryan emperor Ashoka unites the entire Indian subcontinent for the first time.

AD 600 Maya civilization at its height in Mexico.
AD 632 Death of the prophet Mohammed; the Islamic religion is well established in Arabia.

Great Wall of China

2600 BC Construction of the great pyramid of King Khufu at Giza, one of the largest building projects of the ancient world, is begun.

c.753 BC The city of Rome is founded. The left-hand figure represents the great city.

c.220 BC Construction work on the Great Wall of China is begun.

1500–1000

In Egypt, music is played in temples, at home, and for feasts, processions, and funeral ceremonies. Many of the instruments, including large harps, are based on Mesopotamian ones. There are also double-reed pipes, in which one pipe sounds a single, continuous note called a drone and the other plays the tune, possibly using a scale based on the drone note. Most of these instruments are played by women and girls. The Egyptians also invent metal trumpets, which are probably used for signaling.

Ancient Egyptian flautist, c.1400 BC

950

King Solomon's temple in Jerusalem is dedicated. Music plays an important part in the religious ceremonies of the Jews. According to the Second Book of Chronicles in the Bible, the temple dedication ceremony is accompanied by singing, together with music provided by 120 priests playing trumpets. This large group is joined by an orchestra of musicians, who play harps, cymbals, and a variety of other instruments.

700

The Greeks use music in all areas of life, not just religious ceremonies or special occasions. Many of our words used in music come from Greek terms, including "music" itself, which comes from the Greek word *mousike*, meaning the arts of music, dance, and poetry. Words such as "orchestra," "harmony," and "guitar" also come from ancient Greek.

Harpist from Egyptian tomb painting, c.1400 BC. Large harps like this were used in temple rituals and funeral processions. Our knowledge of instruments like this comes from paintings and from discoveries such as the tomb of the pharaoh Tutankhamun.

700

In the Arab lands, the caliphs employ numerous musicians, many of whom become famous throughout the Muslim world. The music and instruments are like those of Mesopotamia.

Persian musicians use a range of instruments, including trumpets, drums, and stringed instruments played with a bow.

900

Music in two or more parts begins to be performed. A second, third, or fourth melody is sung above or below the plainsong or chant.

1000–1599
Medieval music

IN THIS PERIOD music became more elaborate, and composers explored ways of expressing a range of different emotions. To begin with, musicians began to add more complex melodies to the simple chants of the monks. The result was polyphonic music, music written in several parts. An accurate system of writing music down was also developed. In the 13th century, music became even more elaborate. In forms such as the madrigal, different words could be sung at the same time. But religious changes in the 16th century brought demands for vocal music in which the words could be heard more clearly. As a result, church music became simpler once more. Meanwhile, instrumental music was also developing. The first instrumental form, a dance called the estampie, appeared in about 1300.

1000

Wandering minstrels entertain people throughout Europe. They sing songs, often accompanying themselves on stringed instruments, such as harps (played by plucking the strings) and viols (played with a bow).

1030

Guido d'Arezzo (c.990–c.1050), an Italian monk, devises the staff. Notes occupy lines and spaces; clef signs indicate the overall pitch. This system is the basis of the precise notation used today. Guido also invents a system of teaching music in which the notes are given the names *ut (do), re, mi, fa, sol, la.*

1100

Troubadours in France begin to sing songs of courtly love, probably unaccompanied. This trend spreads across Europe during the 12th and 13th centuries.

A troubadour, from a medieval illuminated manuscript

1473

The first complete piece of music is printed; before this time each piece of music had to be copied out by hand. Printing increases the demand for music by the general public, rather than the church and the nobility. This makes composers more interested in writing simple, popular music, and also in producing instrumental music for amateurs to play. As a result, new instrumental styles begin to emerge – particularly for keyboard instruments and the lute.

16th-century lutenist

1514

The Flemish composer Josquin des Prez (c.1440–1521) writes the mass *Missa "Pange Lingua,"* a profound expression of religious belief. With his masses, motets, and songs, Josquin is considered the greatest composer of the age, blending words and music in beautiful and often highly emotional settings. He was named "the Prince of Music" by his contemporaries.

1550

The Italian composer Giovanni Palestrina (1525–94) is a master of polyphonic music in his masses, motets, and psalms. This sacred music is restrained in style. A similar mastery is shown by the English composer Thomas Tallis (c.1505–85) in his famous work *Spem in alium*, composed in 40 separate parts for eight five-voice choirs. It may have been written for the 40th birthday of Queen Elizabeth I in 1573.

Giovanni Palestrina

Wandering minstrel

THE CHANGING WORLD

1000 Gunpowder is first used in warfare in China.
1095 The Pope calls for a crusade, or holy war, against the Muslims who control Jerusalem.
1192 The Japanese emperor appoints the first shogun (great general). The shoguns will wield great power in Japan during the next few centuries.

Crusaders

1206 Mongol leader Genghis Khan begins to conquer large areas of Asia.
1337 England declares war on France, the start of the Hundred Years War.
1347 The black death, an outbreak of bubonic plague, spreads from Asia to Europe, eventually killing about one third of the people of Europe.

Black rat, carrier of the plague

1420 The dome of Florence cathedral is built, and the artistic Renaissance begins.

Early printing press

1455 A German goldsmith called Johannes Gutenberg uses movable type to produce the first large printed book, an edition of the Bible.

1100

The portative organ, a pipe organ small enough to be carried about, becomes popular, probably to accompany singing. It later develops into the positive organ, a larger instrument that can be placed on a table.

1170

The first known composer, the French monk Léonin, compiles the *Magnus Liber*, a great book containing two-part plainsong for all the feasts of the church year. Another French monk, Pérotin, revises the *Magnus Liber* in the early 13th century.

13th-century plainsong manuscript

1250

The song *Sumer is icumen in* shows how polyphonic singing has developed in England. It is a round for four voices, in which the performers sing the same tune and words but enter one after the other. There are also lower parts for two more singers. This popular round is still sung today.

Group of viol players

1450

The French composer Guillaume Dufay (c.1400–74) writes the mass *Se la face ay pale*. In this and other masses, Dufay uses the same theme (not always a sacred melody) as the basis for all five sections of the mass. The result is the first large, unified piece of music.

Guillaume Dufay

1400

Kings, princes, nobles, abbots, towns, and even ships have their own bands to provide music for ceremonies and social occasions. There are two kinds of bands. Loud ensembles contain trumpets and harsh reed instruments such as shawms (early oboes); soft ensembles include strings, such as harps, viols, and lutes, keyboard instruments, and softer winds such as flutes and recorders. The bands often play instrumental versions of vocal music, with upper parts played, often improvised, over a basic melody.

1587

The first concertos, by the Italian composer Andrea Gabrieli (c.1510–86) and his nephew Giovanni Gabrieli (c.1553–1612), are published. These pieces are for contrasting groups of singers or instrumentalists who "compete" against each other.

1599

Englishman Thomas Morley (1557–1602) publishes the *First Booke of Consort Lessons*. Consorts – groups of instruments – have become popular by this time; Morley's is the first book to specify which instruments should be used. It contains pieces (not all by Morley) for two viols, flute, lute, and two forms of guitar called the cittern and pandora.

| Pipe and drum | Viol | Bass Recorder | Lute | Treble Recorder |

1600–1749
Baroque music

THE FIRST PUBLIC opera house opened in the 17th century and many composers began to write operas, oratorios, and cantatas (unstaged dramatic works). As a result, vocal music became more dramatic, with a strong emphasis on the words. Instrumental music developed greatly, with composers devising many new orchestral forms, such as the dance suite, the concerto for solo instruments and orchestra, and the symphony. Composers also expanded the use of tonality, the shift from one key to another, and created an ornate style of music that complements the elaborate baroque architecture of the period. Much of this music was written for violins, rather than the older viols. Similarly, the newly invented piano began to rival the harpsichord by the end of the period. These instruments also inspired composers to write the first chamber music.

1600

Musicians at the court in Florence, Italy

In vocal music, a new style becomes popular – single melodies sung by one singer with instrumental accompaniment. This style is used in the earliest operas. The lack of other parts is remedied by the use of continuo, a style of accompaniment on the lute, harpsichord, or organ, in which the performer plays a written bass line and improvises chords to complete the music.

1615

Sonata for three violins, by the Italian composer Giovanni Gabrieli (c.1553–1612), is published. The term "sonata" has been in use since the previous century to signify any instrumental piece, as opposed to a "cantata," which is sung. Gabrieli's sonata heralds a new meaning for the term: a piece in a set form for a solo instrument or a small group.

Gabrieli also wrote music for wind groups.

1715

The Italian violin maker Antonio Stradivari (1644–1737), known as Stradivarius, is at the height of his powers. His violins – and also violas and cellos – have never been surpassed in their richness of tone. Stradivarius was taught by another great violin maker, Niccolò Amati (1596–1684).

Stradivarius with one of his violins

1709

Early piano

The piano is invented in Italy by Bartolomeo Cristofori (1655–1731). The full name is pianoforte, meaning soft-loud, because it can play both softly and loudly, unlike the harpsichord, which cannot easily change its volume.

1720

In his Partitas and Sonatas for solo violin and his Suites for solo cello, the great German composer Johann Sebastian Bach (1685–1750) produces the first important solo music for non-keyboard instruments. The works are still played today.

Baroque cellist

1722

J.S. Bach produces the first book of *The Well-Tempered Clavier*. A second book follows in 1738–42. These are two sets of 24 preludes and fugues for a solo keyboard instrument (originally the clavichord or harpsichord, although they are now also played on the piano). The preludes and fugues are written in all 12 major and 12 minor keys, showing how a particular keyboard tuning, or temperament, could be made suitable for the complete major-minor system of 24 keys.

18th-century harpsichord player

THE CHANGING WORLD

1600 The East India Company is chartered by Queen Elizabeth I. The company is granted exclusive rights to exploration in the East Indies.
1609 Italian scientist Galileo Galilei looks at the heavens with a telescope; he sees that the Sun, not the Earth, is at the center of the Solar System.

East India officer figure

1618 The Thirty Years War breaks out, involving nearly all of Europe.
1620 The Mayflower sets sail from England to America, carrying the first European settlers.
1642 Dutch navigator Abel Tasman sails to Australian waters and is the first European to visit Tasmania and New Zealand.

Late 1600s The discoveries of Isaac Newton transform mathematics and the science of physics.
1701 British inventor Jethro Tull introduces the seed drill, one of a number of machines that transform agriculture in Europe.
1725 Learning flourishes in China. The *Gujin tushu jicheng*, a huge encyclopedia with 10,000 chapters, is commissioned by the Qing emperor Yongzheng.

Isaac Newton's telescope

1637

The first public opera house opens in Venice, Italy. Formerly a court entertainment, opera begins to become popular with ordinary people. The new audience demands more realistic stories than the mythological subjects previously used. Also in Venice, the Italian composer Claudio Monteverdi (1567–1643) produces the early opera, *The Coronation of Poppaea* in 1642. This work is based on the life of the Roman emperor Nero.

1662

Jean-Baptiste Lully (1632–87), an Italian born composer, becomes director of music at the court of French king Louis XIV. Lully leads a large orchestra and develops greater contrasts of sound in the instrumental music that he composes for dramatic scenes in his many operas and ballets.

1664

The English composer Henry Purcell (1659–95) is appointed organist at Westminster Abbey, London. During the coming years he will write a series of religious works and numerous pieces to entertain the court of the English king and queen. He will also compose the first famous English opera, *Dido and Aeneas* (1689).

1681

The Italian composer Arcangelo Corelli (1653–1713) pioneers the trio sonata. This form is for two violins and bass viol, plus keyboard continuo, and usually has four movements. Corelli becomes a renowned violinist, and his works soon influence other composers.

Early chamber ensemble

Elias Haussmann, senior musician in Bach's orchestra

1725

The Italian composer Antonio Vivaldi (1678–1741) composes *The Four Seasons*, a set of four violin concertos that portray the events of the seasons, such as shivering and falling on ice in winter. In his lifetime, Vivaldi writes about 350 concertos for a solo instrument and orchestra. These are mainly for the violin, but also for the flute, bassoon, oboe, cello, and a range of other instruments.

1742

George Frideric Handel (1685–1759), who was born in Germany but lived and worked mainly in England, composes the famous oratorio *Messiah*. An oratorio is a setting of a religious text for solo singers, choir, and orchestra, usually performed without costumes or scenery in a church or concert hall. *Messiah* follows two great passions (oratorios based on the story of Christ's suffering and death): the *St. John Passion* (1724) and *St. Matthew Passion* (1727) by J.S. Bach.

1750–1824
Classical music

MUSIC ENTERED THE classical age in the late 18th century. During this period, composers, above all Haydn and Mozart, established the main forms of instrumental music – the sonata, string quartet, concerto, and symphony. There was also a change in musical style. The interweaving lines of baroque music mostly disappeared, replaced by strong melodies that were reworked and expanded in tuneful phrases, with contrasts of sound and constant, well organized movement from one key to another. In the early 19th century, composers such as Beethoven and Schubert developed these orchestral forms. Instrumental music was dominated by the piano, which evolved into a highly expressive instrument, inspiring composers to produce great solo works. Vocal music – opera, oratorio, and song – became more and more dramatic and poetic during the period.

1751

Two clarinets are added to the orchestra of a theater in Paris. This marks the beginning of the modern symphony orchestra, with flutes, oboes, clarinets, bassoons, horns, trumpets, and drums. This instrumentation becomes standard by the end of the century.

1761

The Austrian composer Joseph Haydn (1732–1809) is appointed music director to the Hungarian nobleman Prince Paul Esterházy. Under the patronage of the Prince, and his successor Nicholas, Haydn writes four-movement symphonies in a variety of styles, greatly developing the form. Haydn composes some 104 symphonies in his lifetime.

Esterháza, the home of Haydn's patron

1762

The opera *Orfeo ed Euridice* (*Orpheus and Eurydice*) by the German composer Christoph Willibald Gluck (1714–87) is first performed in Vienna. This and later operas by Gluck reform opera by making more use of music to support and enhance the drama.

1798

Toward the end of his life Haydn moves to Vienna, where he composes *The Creation*, an oratorio based on the Book of Genesis and the poem *Paradise Lost* by the English poet John Milton. The work continues the tradition of oratorio developed during the Baroque period, and is Haydn's most successful piece in his lifetime. In 1801 he follows this with *The Seasons*, another oratorio based on the work of an English poet, James Thompson.

Haydn composing *The Creation*

1796

Public concerts continue to play an important part in the musical life of Europe. The ticket shown left comes from one of a series of public concerts held in London.

Haydn writes a concerto for the new keyed trumpet, which can produce more notes than the older instruments.

Keyed trumpet

1805

Italian violinist and composer Nicolò Paganini (1782–1840) composes *24 Caprices* for solo violin. In these and his later violin concertos, Paganini exhibits a virtuoso style of playing for which he is famous. One of the caprices, in A minor, is later used by Brahms, Rachmaninov, and other composers as the basis for sets of variations.

1811

The Austrian composer Franz Schubert (1797–1828) writes the first of over 600 *Lieder* (songs) for singer and piano. These moving settings of poems show Schubert's wonderful sense of melody, as do his orchestral and chamber works. Among the most famous are the Symphony no. 8 in B minor (the "Unfinished") and the *Trout* Quintet (1819), named after a song used in one movement as a basis for variations.

Schubert and his friends at a musical evening

THE CHANGING WORLD

1765 Scotsman James Watt designs the first efficient steam engine.
1781 The American Revolutionary War ends, bringing the end of British rule in North America and preparing the way for the founding of the United States.
British uniform of the Revolutionary War

1789 The French Revolution begins with the storming of the Bastille prison in Paris. This prison is a symbol of royal power.
1792 The French monarchy is replaced by the republic.
1804 Napoleon crowns himself emperor of France and begins a series of military campaigns in Europe.

1814 British engineer George Stephenson builds steam locomotives for railroads in England.

One of Stephenson's locomotives

1815 The British and Prussians defeat French emperor Napoleon at the Battle of Waterloo.
1819 The state of Singapore is founded by Stamford Raffles.
1821 The South American states of Bolivia and Peru win independence.

1763

The German composer Johann Christian Bach (1735–82) develops the concerto in works for the newly invented piano and orchestra, following the example of the harpsichord concertos of his father, J. S. Bach, and elder brother Carl Philipp Emanuel Bach (1714–88).

1772

Following a childhood as a musical prodigy, including an opera composed at the age of 12, the Austrian composer Wolfgang Amadeus Mozart (1756–91), still only 16, produces four symphonies that establish him as a leading composer. He will write 41 symphonies in his lifetime. Haydn meanwhile composes the Symphony no. 45 in F-sharp minor (the "Farewell Symphony"), which ends with the performers leaving the concert platform one by one.

1787

Mozart composes three great operas: *The Marriage of Figaro* (1786), *Don Giovanni* (1787), and *The Magic Flute* (1791). He often uses duets, trios, quartets, and even larger groups of principal singers to enhance the characterization and action, which may be humorous as well as moving and dramatic.

Mozart composing *Don Giovanni*

1781

Haydn develops the string quartet in his Opus 33 quartets. He takes a theme and splits it up, so that each player has an equal role in the music. The form will be further developed by Mozart and German composer Ludwig van Beethoven (1770–1827) in a series of quartets.

1816

The Barber of Seville, an opera by the Italian composer Gioacchino Rossini (1792–1868) is first given in Rome. In this work, Rossini revitalizes opera with tunes that are witty and zestful.

Scene from the *Barber of Seville*

1824

Beethoven reaches the climax of his career with the performance of his last symphony, no. 9 in D minor. A big work for chorus and orchestra, it is the most ambitious of his symphonies, which develop the form to express the most profound human emotions. Among the most famous are no. 3 (the *Eroica*, originally dedicated to Napoleon), no. 5, and no. 6 (the *Pastoral*). Beethoven's other works include five piano concertos, 32 piano sonatas, and the opera *Fidelio*.

Beethoven was one of the greatest composers, who left his mark on nearly every form of music

1825–1874
Romantic music

THE DRAMA AND poetry of Beethoven and Schubert inspired a change in music. More and more composers used music to express emotions and ideas, rather than to explore the formal qualities of the classical era. Many composers still wrote in classical forms, such as the symphony, but they gave them a new intensity. Another development was the popularity of program music, in which events or scenes are portrayed by the instruments. Improvements in instruments enabled these advances to take place. The piano developed the full, rich tone that we know today; brass instruments, now equipped with valves, became capable of a full range of music. The orchestra expanded in size, providing composers with a greater variety of sound.

1830

The French composer Hector Berlioz (1803–69) writes *Symphonie Fantastique* (*Fantastic Symphony*). Subtitled "Episodes in the life of an artist," it is a highly romantic work inspired by the composer's obsessive love for the actress Harriet Smithson, described in the music by a recurring theme. In this and later works, Berlioz greatly develops the expressive use of the orchestra, introducing new instruments, such as the valve trumpet and bass clarinet.

The sea and rock formations that inspired Felix Mendelssohn to write *The Hebrides*

1830

The German composer Felix Mendelssohn (1809–47) writes *The Hebrides* (or *Fingal's Cave*), a masterly depiction of the sea and the magnificent coastal scenery off the northwest coast of Scotland. It is the first important concert overture (a short one-movement orchestral work intended to open a concert).

1848

Liszt introduces the symphonic poem or tone poem, which is a large-scale, one-movement work that describes a nonmusical subject, such as people and events in mythology, history, or literature.

1846

The Hungarian composer Franz Liszt (1811–86), a brilliant pianist, begins a set of *Hungarian Rhapsodies*. These virtuoso piano works introduce the rhapsody, a one-movement work inspired by a general idea or style (in this case by Hungarian folk music). Liszt's works also herald national music (pp. 64–65). This development continues, two years later, with *Kamarinskaya* (*Wedding Song*), an extended orchestral piece based on Russian folk tunes by the Russian composer Mikhail Glinka (1804–57).

Caricature of Liszt at the piano

1853

La Traviata, an opera by the Italian composer Giuseppe Verdi (1813–1901), is first performed. Verdi's operas cover new ground by introducing realistic characters in a wide variety of plots. Verdi follows this with other operas, such as the drama *Aïda* (1871).

Scene from *La Traviata*

1864

The German musician Hans von Bülow (1830–94) becomes conductor of the Munich Opera. As scores become more complex, it is more important to have a conductor to take charge of performances. Composers such as Berlioz and Wagner usually conducted their own music, but von Bülow is the first to specialize in conducting others' works, and makes concert tours in Europe and the US.

1869

The Russian composer Peter Ilyich Tchaikovsky (1840–93) composes his first orchestral masterpiece, the *Romeo and Juliet Fantasy Overture*. It is typical of Tchaikovsky's highly tuneful, colorful, and emotional music, which achieves lasting fame.

Ballet version of *Romeo and Juliet*

THE CHANGING WORLD

Gold nugget

1848 Poverty and social unrest lead to revolutions in many European countries.
1849 Gold is discovered in California; thousands travel westward to make their fortunes. The gold rush leads to the growth of cities such as San Francisco.

c.1850 Jeans are invented in California.
1854 A treaty is signed between Japan and the United States, opening up trade between Japan and the West for the first time.
1853 War breaks out in the Crimea in Russia. Turkey, Britain, France, and Sardinia fight

Russia. During this war Englishwoman Florence Nightingale brings proper nursing to the troops for the first time.
1860 King Victor Emmanuel is crowned as the first king of a united Italy. Previously Italy had been divided.

1867 Canada becomes a dominion, a self-governing nation within the British empire.
1871 The many separate German states unite as one country and William I is proclaimed German emperor.

Early light bulb

1874 The American inventor Thomas Edison and British inventor Joseph Swan begin work on the first electric light bulbs. In 20 years' time, electric lighting will become common in Europe and America.

1830

The Polish composer Frederic Chopin (1810–49) composes the *Revolutionary Etude*, a stunning piano piece of turbulent emotion. Chopin, who wrote almost all of his music for the piano, takes piano playing into new realms with his brilliant technique. Most of Chopin's works are short, melodic pieces that often make use of adventurous harmony.

Chopin took full advantage of developments in piano making that made the instrument easier to play and gave it a richer sound

1835

The German composer Robert Schumann (1810–56) writes *Carnaval*, a set of descriptive pieces for the piano. It is followed in 1838 by another set, *Scenes from Childhood*, containing the famous piece, *Reverie*, and in 1845 by the Piano Concerto in A minor. All are typical of Schumann's lyrical and intimate music, romantic in style, but not overdramatic.

Robert Schumann with his wife, Clara, one of the most famous pianists of the time

1843

The German composer Richard Wagner (1813–83) composes *The Flying Dutchman*, one of several operas, or music dramas, as Wagner calls them. These works, mostly based on legends, revolutionize music by using recurring motifs (short themes representing things or characters) in a continually developing musical structure.

1835

The valve horn begins to replace the natural horn in the scores of composers such as Wagner and Schumann. It helps composers create a much more dramatic and intensely expressive sound.

Johannes Brahms on his way to his favorite haunt, an inn called the Red Hedgehog

1874

Wagner's music dramas culminate in the great four opera cycle, *The Ring of the Nibelungen*, which he completes after working on it for some 26 years.

1874

The German composer Johannes Brahms (1833–97) composes *Variations on the St. Anthony Chorale*. In this and his symphonies, concertos, and sonatas, Brahms continues composing in the classical forms, employing a romantic style but rejecting the musical depictions and descriptions of program music.

1875–1899

National music

ROMANTIC MUSIC AND opera continued to develop in the late 19th century. But the romantic tradition, which was created largely by composers from Germany and Austria, did not appeal to everyone. Many composers from other European countries wanted to celebrate national qualities in their music, so they began to produce works that portrayed the scenery, history, and literature of their homelands. This music often made use of folk music, and it developed mainly in Scandinavia, Britain, eastern Europe, and Russia. Toward the end of the century, a new kind of music, impressionism, developed in France. Inspired by the style of impressionist painting, it contains beautiful and unusual sounds that suggest subjects and feelings quite different from the intense and dramatic nature of romantic music.

1875

The opera *Carmen*, by French composer Georges Bizet (1838–75), shocks audiences with its realism and its hot-blooded but tragic story. It soon becomes world famous and is still one of the most popular operas.

Maria Ewing as Carmen

1875

The flag of Norway

Norwegian composer Edvard Grieg (1843–1907) writes *Peer Gynt* as incidental music to Henrik Ibsen's play of the same name. Grieg also writes pieces such as the *Norwegian Dances* and *Wedding Day at Troldhaugen*. In works like these, he establishes a Norwegian school of music. Grieg's other works include a famous piano concerto, many piano works, and numerous songs.

1888

The French composer Erik Satie (1866–1925) writes *Gymnopédies*, a set of three piano pieces of original and utter simplicity that gives them long-lasting appeal. They are later orchestrated by Debussy. Satie's piano music and ballet scores have a lasting influence on French composers, particularly Debussy and Ravel.

Caricature of Erik Satie

1892

Tchaikovsky writes the ballet *The Nutcracker*, which has its first performance in St. Petersburg. The ballet is based on a fairytale, and features a battle between the Nutcracker and the King of Mice.

1892

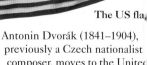

The US fla[g]

Antonin Dvořák (1841–1904), previously a Czech nationalist composer, moves to the United States, where he composes the *American* string quartet and the famous Symphony no. 9 in E minor, *From The New World*, which contains elements of Czech and American folk music.

THE CHANGING WORLD

1876 The British proclaim Queen Victoria Empress of India.
1876 Working in the United States, the Scottish inventor Alexander Graham Bell invents the telephone.
1877 American inventor Thomas Edison invents the first record player.
1881 Britain defeated by Transvaal in the First Boer War in southern Africa.
1885 The Canadian Pacific Railway opens.

1885 German engineer Karl Benz is the first to make and sell motor cars.
1886 The Statue of Liberty is erected on Bedloe's Island at the entrance to the harbor in New York.
1889 Gustave Eiffel designs the Eiffel Tower for the Paris World Exhibition.
1894 Italian inventor Guglielmo Marconi makes the first radio transmissions in his attic in Bologna.
1899 The Second Boer War breaks out in southern Africa.

Statue of Liberty, New York

Eiffel Tower, Paris

Transmitter

1880

Russian composer Peter Ilyich Tchaikovsky writes the *1812 Overture*, a famous piece of program music containing fireworks and cannon. The work, which incorporates both the French and Russian national anthems, celebrates Russia's victory over the French emperor Napoleon in 1812.

1880

Czech Bedrich Smetana (1824–84) writes *Vltava*, a portrayal of the River Vltava in the Czech Republic. It is the best known of a set of symphonic poems called *Má Vlast* (*My Country*), in which Smetana founds a national school of Czech music.

Czech landscape that inspired Smetana

1888

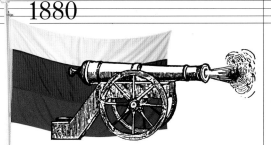

Gustav Mahler (1860–1911), a Bohemian composer living in Austria, writes the first of his ten symphonies, which continued and developed the romantic tradition. They are works on a grand scale, the eighth symphony being known as the *Symphony of a Thousand* because of the vast forces required to perform it.

Mahler was well known as a conductor

1888

Verdi's opera *Otello*, composed the previous year and based on William Shakespeare's play *Othello*, is given its first US performance in New York. This brings Verdi's greatest work recognition outside his own country, greatly enhancing the reputation of Italian music.

Placido Domingo as Otello

1894

French composer Claude Debussy (1862–1918) writes *L'après-midi d'un faune*, which establishes impressionist music.

1898

The sousaphone is designed by American band-master John Philip Sousa (1854 –1932). It is carried by placing it over the shoulder.

1899

Finnish composer Jean Sibelius (1865–1957) writes *Finlandia*, an orchestral work that establishes a Finnish school of music. It portrays his native Finland, but without using the style or tunes of folk music.

The flag of Finland

1899

British composer Edward Elgar (1857–1934) writes *Enigma Variations* for orchestra. Each variation is a musical portrait of one of Elgar's friends, except the final one, which represents the composer himself. It is the first important British work for over 200 years, and founds a British school of music. A series of works, including two symphonies and several choral pieces, follow during the first 20 years of the century.

1900–1939
Revolutionary music

WITH THE DAWN of the new century, romantic composers strove for more and more intense effects. Eventually they took music to the point at which tonality, the use of keys developed over 200 years, broke down. Some composers began to write revolutionary and often exciting music in two or more keys at once, producing strange harmonies. They also combined instruments and rhythms in new ways. Then, in 1921, the Austrian composer Schoenberg introduced twelve-tone or serial music. A twelve-tone piece is based on a series of twelve notes of the chromatic scale instead of the seven-note major and minor scales of traditional tonal music. But many listeners found this music unpleasant, and other composers continued to write in the romantic tradition.

Sergei Rachmaninov

1901

The Russian composer Sergei Rachmaninov (1873–1943) composes Piano Concerto no. 2 in C minor, a famous concerto firmly in the old romantic tradition. Rachmaninov is a superb pianist, and plays his concertos and solo piano works in concerts and, later, in the recording studio, keeping the romantic style of music alive in the 20th century.

1906

Isolated from the European mainstream, the American Charles Ives (1874–1954) composes *The Unanswered Question* and *Central Park in the Dark*. These orchestral works are revolutionary – sections of the orchestra play different kinds of music that combine in ways never heard before. Ives pioneers the simultaneous use of different keys, rhythms, and sound textures.

Central Park, New York

1920

Stravinsky (1882–1971) composes *Pulcinella*, a ballet based on music by Giovanni Pergolesi (1710–36) and other baroque composers, and *Symphonies of Wind Instruments*. In these works, Stravinsky pioneers a neoclassical music that looks back to past styles and forms, but reinterprets them using 20th-century advances in music.

Vanessa Redgrave in *The Threepenny Opera*

1916

The British composer Gustav Holst (1874–1934) completes *The Planets*, an orchestral suite portraying the mythological gods after whom the planets are named. The work's seven movements portray Mars, Venus, Mercury, Jupiter, Saturn, Uranus, and Neptune. It is a powerful reflection on the changes that were taking place in English music.

1925

Early recording session

Electrical sound recording is introduced, producing records of a much higher quality than the old acoustic system. Many conductors take their orchestras to the studio, where the players crowd around the microphones. Records contain only a few minutes of music, but attract many new listeners.

1928

The German Kurt Weill (1900–50) writes *The Threepenny Opera*. It is one of several operas in a unique style that combines jazz and cabaret styles with unusual changes of harmony.

1934

The Russian composer Dmitri Shostakovich (1906–75) composes the opera *Lady Macbeth of Mtsensk*, and is criticized by the Russian authorities for producing "discordant and confused" music. Shostakovich atones with his Symphony no. 5 in D minor (1937), composed on more traditional lines, but continues to develop his own style in later symphonies and string quartets.

Scene from *Lady Macbeth of Mtsensk* by Shostakovich

Revolutionary poster

THE CHANGING WORLD

1903 American inventors Wilbur and Orville Wright make the first powered flights in an airplane.
1914 World War I begins in Europe and will continue for four years.
1917 Revolution breaks out in Russia. The Bolsheviks (Communists) take power and in the following year a new constitution is declared and the Tsar is killed.
1919 Scientist Ernest Rutherford splits the atom for the first time.

Gandhi and his followers

1930 Indian leader Mohandas K. Gandhi sets out on his "salt march," one of his protests against British rule in India.
1936 The first public television service opens in Britain.
1930s The tape recorder is developed in Germany.

Early reel-to-reel tape recorder

1908

The French composer Maurice Ravel (1875–1937) composes the brilliant piano work *Gaspard de la Nuit* and the comparatively simple piano duet *Mother Goose*, which, like other piano works, he later orchestrates with a highly imaginative range of tone color. In his works, Ravel extends the impressionism of Debussy, often using it in classical forms.

1908

The Austrian composer Arnold Schoenberg (1874–1951) develops atonal music, in which harmony changes so much that it loses the sense of a key center and is no longer tonal. He uses atonality fully in *Erwartung* (*Expectation*, 1909), a vision of a nightmare for soprano and orchestra. The atonal technique will be used by many later composers.

1909

The German composer Richard Strauss (1864–1949) finishes the opera *Elektra*, which is given its first performance in Dresden. In works like *Elektra* and the opera *Salome* (1905), Strauss creates operas typified by their strong heroines.

A scene from the opera *Salome*, by Richard Strauss

1916

The Spanish composer Manuel de Falla (1876–1946) writes *Nights in the Gardens of Spain* for piano and orchestra. This is a three-movement work, which the composer describes as a series of "symphonic impressions". In it, de Falla combines impressionism with Spanish national music to portray the beauty of the gardens at the Alhambra palace in Granada, southern Spain.

1911

The Russian composer Igor Stravinsky (1882–1971) writes the ballet *Petrushka*, followed in 1913 by *The Rite of Spring*. These works develop the technique of polytonality (the use of two or more keys at once) as well as unusual and powerful rhythms. The savage music of *The Rite of Spring* provokes a riot at its first performance in Paris.

Igor Stravinsky works on one of his scores. He wrote many orchestral works, including a number of successful ballets

1935

In America, George Gershwin (1898–1937), a highly successful composer of popular songs, turns to opera with *Porgy and Bess*. He combines elements of blues and spirituals with the European operatic tradition in a tuneful and highly dramatic work that rivals Bizet's *Carmen*.

Scene from *Porgy and Bess*

1936

The Russian Sergei Prokofiev (1891–1953) composes the ballet *Romeo and Juliet*, a romantic and dramatic work, and the famous children's work *Peter and the Wolf*, in which characters in a fairy tale are identified by different instruments of the orchestra. Two orchestral suites are later compiled from the music of *Romeo and Juliet*. In these and other works, Prokofiev composes attractive melodies distinguished by sudden and unusual key changes.

1940–2000
Modern music

UNLIKE PREVIOUS CENTURIES, when music evolved in one main direction, music in the 20th century has split into more and more different styles. In the 1950s, Stockhausen and Boulez developed the twelve-tone method of Schoenberg into a very strict and complex music called total serialism. At the same time, John Cage in the United States was writing music in which notes are randomly selected. A reaction to these ideas led to minimalist music, a style featuring rhythmic and melodic repetition that dominated the 1970s and 1980s, and to polystylistic music, which combines several styles in the same piece. As the century draws to a close, these directions meet in a style often called postmodernism.

The peaks of the Appalachian Mountains

1944

In the United States, Aaron Copland (1900–90) becomes the foremost composer of an American national school with music for the ballet *Appalachian Spring*. This work is a set of variations on a traditional hymn called "Simple Gifts."

1945

The British composer Benjamin Britten (1913–76) writes the

Benjamin Britten (right)

opera *Peter Grimes*, a dramatic story of a fisherman, containing orchestral interludes that vividly portray the sea. It uses traditional musical styles, as does *The Young Person's Guide to the Orchestra* (1946), which features all the orchestral instruments playing separately, in sections, and all together.

1987

The American composer John Adams (b. 1947) writes the opera *Nixon in China* followed in 1991 by *The Death of Klinghoffer*. In these operas, which are both about contemporary political events, Adams develops the techniques of minimalism to create powerful, almost romantic, music.

President Richard M. Nixon visits China in 1972

1989

The British composer Mark-Anthony Turnage (b. 1960) writes *Three Screaming Popes*, an orchestral work based on paintings by Francis Bacon (1909–92). The music is powerfully rhythmic in places, reflecting Turnage's interest in the strong rhythms of jazz and rock music.

1989

The Estonian composer Arvo Pärt (b. 1935) writes *Miserere* for five voices, chorus, and orchestra. In profoundly religious works like *Miserere, Cantus in Memoriam Benjamin Britten*, and *St. John Passion*, Pärt produces music of great stillness and utter simplicity, recalling medieval music in its haunting beauty.

Arvo Pärt

Detail of Francis Bacon's *Study after Pope Innocent X by Velasquez*

THE CHANGING WORLD

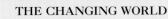

1945 World War II ends with the surrender of Germany and Japan.
1947 India becomes independent from the British and the separate state of Pakistan is formed.
1957 The Soviet Union launches *Sputnik I*, the first artificial satellite to go into orbit around the earth.
1963 President John F. Kennedy is assassinated in Dallas, Texas.
1969 United States astronaut Neil Armstrong is the first person to land on the moon.

Sputnik I

1973 In Sydney, Australia, the opera house is completed after 14 years of construction work.

Sydney Opera House

1979 The audio CD is launched, bringing digital recordings into the home for the first time.
1989 The Berlin Wall is taken down, signaling the end of Communist rule in eastern Europe.
1991 Slovenia and Croatia declare independence from Yugoslavia, beginning a chain of events that lead to war in the Balkans.
1994 Multiracial elections are held in South Africa; Nelson Mandela becomes president.

Audio CD

1948

Frenchman Olivier Messiaen (1913–92) composes the *Turangalîla Symphony*, a vast orchestral work that portrays love. Messiaen uses all kinds of methods to create unusual harmonies and structures, including Indian rhythms and bird songs, all expressed in a wide range of tone color, featuring the Ondes Martenot, an early electronic instrument.

1956

The German composer Karlheinz Stockhausen (b. 1928) writes *Gesang der Jünglinge (Song of the Youths)*, the first masterpiece of electronic music. It is a tape recording of a chorister's voice, often transformed by ingenious tape manipulation, and pure sounds made electronically. It is played back on five loudspeakers.

1957

In the United States, Leonard Bernstein (1918–90) composes *West Side Story*, a musical that sets the conflict of Shakespeare's *Romeo and Juliet* in mid-20th century New York.

1961

Ligeti's new type of score

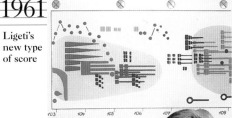

In Hungary, György Ligeti (b. 1923) writes *Atmosphères*, an orchestral work using a pictorial method of indicating sounds. It has a new kind of orchestral sound, without specific melody or harmony.

1975

American composer Philip Glass (b. 1937) develops minimalist music with the opera *Einstein on the Beach*. In this and later operas about the Indian leader Mahatma Gandhi and ancient Egyptian king Akhnaten, Glass uses minimalist techniques to form large musical structures.

Scene from Glass's *Akhnaten*

1967

The Japanese composer Toru Takemitsu (b. 1930) writes *November Steps* for biwa, shakuhachi, and orchestra. The biwa, a lute, and shakuhachi, a bamboo flute, are Japanese folk instruments, and Takemitsu merges their sounds and ways of playing music with the sounds and instruments of the classical Western orchestra.

Bamboo flute

Japanese lute

1964

In America, Terry Riley (b. 1935) pioneers minimalist music with *In C*, a work for any instruments and of no particular length. The players continually repeat a short phrase of music over and over again before moving on to another, and work their way through 53 phrases. The phrases combine to produce music of static harmony that is constantly shifting in rhythm and in which short melodies form at random.

1994

The British premiere of *De Materie* (1988), a postmodern work by the Dutch composer Louis Andriessen (b. 1939), shows him to be a leading composer of the 1990s. The French composer and conductor Pierre Boulez (b. 1925) also premieres *...explosante-fixe* (1993) in Britain. With its use of computer technology, *...explosante-fixe* points the way to the musical future.

Pierre Boulez is well known as a conductor of 20th-century music

2000

The late 1990s are likely to see progress in two developments that have already begun and are long overdue in modern music. The first is the influence of recent popular music, including jazz, on younger composers who have grown up with it and are more familiar with this music than most of their forebears. What they could bring to classical music is not so much the actual style of playing popular music but the strong intensity of that music. The second is advanced technology. The computer is still largely absent from the concert platform even though it has invaded many other walks of life. What this technology could bring is impossible to forecast, but it should greatly expand our experience of music.

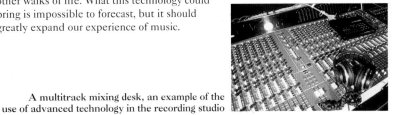

A multitrack mixing desk, an example of the use of advanced technology in the recording studio

A–Z of composers

○ **Adams, John** (b. 1947) American composer John Adams began by writing minimalist music, such as *Shaker Loops* for strings. He later developed this and other styles with the choral work *Harmonium*, the orchestral work *Grand Pianola Music*, and the opera *Nixon in China*.

○ **Albéniz, Isaac** (1860–1909) A Spanish composer of music in the Spanish national style, Albéniz is known for *Iberia*, a set of piano pieces portraying the regions of his native country.

○ **Bach, Johann Sebastian** (1685–1750) The German musician J.S. Bach is often regarded as the greatest composer of the baroque era. His major works include the six *Brandenburg Concertos* for various soloists and orchestra; the keyboard works *Goldberg Variations* and *The Well-Tempered Clavier*; and choral works *St. John Passion*, *St. Matthew Passion*, and *Mass in B minor*.

○ **Barber, Samuel** (1910–81) This American composer is best known for the beautiful piece *Adagio for Strings*, originally the slow movement of a string quartet but later arranged by Barber for string orchestra.

J.S. Bach

○ **Bartók, Béla** (1881–1945) Born in Hungary, Bartók lived in the United States from 1940. He developed classical forms in an individual, logical way in six string quartets, three piano concertos, and two violin concertos. He also composed the orchestral works *Music for Strings, Percussion, and Celesta*, and *Concerto for Orchestra*; and the ballet *The Miraculous Mandarin*.

○ **Beethoven, Ludwig van** (1770–1827) The German composer Beethoven developed classical forms into highly expressive, often dramatic pieces of music. He became totally deaf, but continued to compose. He wrote nine symphonies, of which the third (*Eroica*), fifth, sixth (*Pastoral*), and ninth (*Choral*) are

Hector Berlioz

best known; five piano concertos, of which the fifth (*Emperor*) is the most popular; and 32 piano sonatas – the eighth (*Pathétique*) and fourteenth (*Moonlight*) are favorites.

○ **Berg, Alban** (1885–1935) Berg was an Austrian composer who developed the twelve-tone method of composition into highly expressive music, often with links to the past or other traditions. He incorporated a passage from a Bach chorale into his violin concerto, and jazz into the opera *Lulu*.

○ **Berlioz, Hector** (1803–69) Frenchman Hector Berlioz was a pioneer of romantic music, and greatly developed the sound of the orchestra. He wrote romantic

symphonies called *Symphonie Fantastique*, *Harold in Italy*, and *Romeo and Juliet*; choral works such as *The Damnation of Faust* and *Requiem*; and the operas *Benvenuto Cellini* and *The Trojans*.

○ **Bizet, Georges** (1838–75) Bizet was a French composer known mainly for his operas *Carmen* (which includes *The Toreador's Song* and several other famous arias) and *The Pearl Fishers*. Bizet also composed the piano duet and orchestral suite *Children's Games*.

○ **Borodin, Alexander** (1833–87) The Russian composer of the opera *Prince Igor*, which contains the well-known choral piece *Polovtsian Dances*, Borodin

Benjamin Britten

Aaron Copland

also wrote two string quartets, of which the second is widely performed.

○ Boulez, Pierre (b. 1925) French composer Pierre Boulez developed the twelve-tone method of Schoenberg into a compositional style called total serialism, as in the vocal work *Le Marteau sans Maître (The Hammer without a Master)*. He later pioneered music using computers and musicians in *Répons* and *...explosante-fixe*.

○ Brahms, Johannes (1833–97) Brahms was born in Hamburg, Germany. He continued to develop classical forms in the romantic period. His compositions include four symphonies, two piano concertos, a violin concerto, the orchestral works *Academic Festival Overture* and *Variations on the St. Anthony Chorale*, and the choral works *A German Requiem* and *Alto Rhapsody*.

○ Britten, Benjamin (1913–76) This British composer is mainly known for his operas, which include *Peter Grimes, Billy Budd*, and *The Turn of the Screw*. His other compositions include the choral work *War Requiem*, the vocal work *Serenade for Tenor, Horn, and Strings*, and *The Young Person's Guide to the Orchestra*, which showcases instruments of the orchestra.

○ Bruckner, Anton (1824–96) The Austrian Anton Bruckner composed large-scale orchestral and religious works, including ten symphonies.

○ Cage, John (1912–92) An American experimental composer of highly unusual

John Cage with part of the score of *Concert for Piano and Orchestra*

works, Cage changed the sound of the piano in *Sonatas and Interludes* and, with *Music of Changes*, investigated music in which the notes occur by chance.

○ Chopin, Frédéric (1810–49) Born in Poland, the virtuoso pianist and composer Chopin lived in France from 1831. Almost all of his works are for the piano, and include sets of waltzes, etudes, nocturnes, and preludes, as well as two piano concertos and three sonatas.

○ Copland, Aaron (1900–90) The music of American composer Copland often makes use of jazz and American folk music. His works include the ballets *Billy the Kid, Rodeo*, and *Appalachian Spring*, and the orchestral work *El Salón México*.

○ Corelli, Arcangelo (1653–1713) Working in his native Italy, Corelli established the sonata as a musical form. He was also a pioneer of the concerto grosso.

○ Couperin, François (1668–1733) Called Couperin the Great to distinguish him from other musical members of his family, this French composer is known mainly for more than 200 harpsichord pieces.

○ Debussy, Claude (1862–1918) French composer Claude Debussy pioneered impressionist music with orchestral works like *Prelude to the Afternoon of a Faun* and *La Mer (The Sea)*, and the piano works *Children's Corner* and two books of *Preludes*.

○ Delius, Frederick (1862–1934) Delius was a British composer who spent much of his life in France. He wrote romantic, poetic music, such as the choral work *Sea Drift*.

Claude Debussy

Dowland, John (1536–1626) The greatest lutenist of his age, Dowland was an English composer of lute music and songs, known mainly for *Lachrimae*, a set of seven pieces for lute and five viols or violins, all based on a single theme.

Dvořák, Antonin (1841–1904) This composer of Czech national music wrote the *Slavonic Dances* for piano duet and also for orchestra. Elements of Czech music also appear in his nine symphonies, of which the ninth *(From the New World)* is most famous, 14 string quartets, a cello concerto, and 14 operas including *Rusalka*.

Elgar, Edward (1857–1934) The British composer Elgar is known mainly for *Enigma Variations*, an orchestral work portraying his friends. His other major works include the oratorio *The Dream of Gerontius*, the five *Pomp and Circumstance* marches for orchestra, the overture *Cockaigne*, two symphonies, and a cello concerto.

Falla, Manuel de (1876–1946) A Spanish composer of music in his country's national style, Falla wrote *Nights in the Gardens of Spain* for piano and orchestra, and the ballets *Love the Magician* and *The Three-Cornered Hat*.

Fauré, Gabriel (1845–1924) Frenchman Gabriel Fauré is best known for the choral *Requiem*, the *Dolly Suite* for piano duet, and the orchestral work *Pavane*.

Field, John (1782–1837) Field, who was born in Ireland but lived in Russia from 1803, invented the short and reflective piano piece called the nocturne. The form was later developed by Chopin.

Gabrieli, Giovanni (c.1556–1612) Italian-born composer Gabrieli became an organist at St. Mark's Cathedral, Venice, and pioneered both the concerto and the sonata. In Venice he produced music such as *Sacrae Symphoniae*, in which the singers and players are divided into groups positioned in different parts of the cathedral – in this dramatic music, the groups sing or play phrases that come from different directions as they answer or echo each other.

Gershwin, George (1898–1937) American composer George Gershwin is known for his tuneful songs for musical

George Frideric Handel

shows. His opera *Porgy and Bess* features the famous song *Summertime*. Gershwin also composed several orchestral works, including *Rhapsody in Blue* and *An American in Paris*.

Gluck, Christoph (1714–87) The German composer Christoph Gluck transformed opera by writing music that was more dramatic and which supported the action taking place. His operas include *Orpheus and Eurydice*, *Alceste*, *Iphigenia in Aulis*, *Armide*, and *Iphigenia in Tauris*.

Grieg, Edvard (1843–1907) Born in Norway, Grieg wrote music in his country's national style. His best-known works include a piano concerto, the *Holberg Suite* for strings, and *Peer Gynt*, incidental music for Ibsen's play. Grieg produced two orchestral suites from the *Peer Gynt* music, which include *In the Hall of the Mountain King* and *Solveig's Song*.

Handel, George Frideric (1685–1759) Handel was born in Germany, but moved to England in 1712. He is known mainly for his operas, such as *Julius Caesar* and *Xerxes*, and his oratorios, especially *Messiah*

(containing the famous *Hallelujah Chorus*) and *Solomon*, which contains the orchestral piece *The Arrival of the Queen of Sheba*. His best known orchestral works are the *Water Music* and *Fireworks Music*, both composed for royal occasions. He also wrote many organ concertos.

Haydn, Joseph (1732–1809) Austrian composer Joseph Haydn pioneered the symphony and the string quartet. He wrote more than 104 numbered symphonies, of which no. 45 (*Farewell*) and no. 94 (*Surprise*) are among the most popular. He also composed about 80 string quartets, the best known being no. 77 – it was named the *Emperor Quartet* for its use of the tune that became the national anthem of Austria and Germany. Other major works by Haydn include the oratorio *The Creation* and a trumpet concerto.

Henze, Hans Werner (b. 1926) Henze is a German composer who uses several different styles and whose music often expresses the composer's political views. He has written several operas, including *Boulevard Solitude* and *The Bassarids*.

Holst, Gustav (1874–1934) This British composer is known mainly for the orchestral suite *The Planets*. He also wrote the overture *Egdon Heath*, the *St. Paul's Suite* for strings, the choral work *Hymn of Jesus*, and the operas *Savitri* and *The Perfect Fool*.

Ives, Charles (1874–1954) American composer Ives wrote progressive music, little of which was known during his

Joseph Haydn

Christoph Gluck

lifetime. His works include the orchestral pieces *The Unanswered Question* and *Three Places in New England*, which paints musical landscapes; the *Concord* sonata for piano; four symphonies; and *Variations on America*, a humorous set of variations on the tune known as *America* or *God Save the Queen*.

○ **Janáček, Leos** (1854–1928) This composer wrote works that make use of Czech folk music. He is known for his operas, which include *Jenufa*, *The Cunning Little Vixen*, *Katya Kabanová*, and *The Makropulos Affair*; the choral work *Glagolitic Mass*; and the orchestral piece *Sinfonietta*, with its exciting brass fanfares.

○ **Liszt, Franz** (1811–86) A Hungarian composer and virtuoso pianist, Liszt invented the symphonic poem, and composed 13 of them. He also raised piano playing to new heights with piano works such as the 19 *Hungarian Rhapsodies*, of which no. 2 in C-sharp minor is famous, and the popular *Liebestraum no. 3*.

○ **Lully, Jean-Baptiste** (1632–87) Born in Italy, Lully lived most of his life in France. He developed both ballet and opera, and is known for the operas *Alceste* and *Armide*.

○ **Machaut, Guillaume de** (c.1300–77) A French composer, Machaut wrote the *Messe de Nostre Dame (Mass of Our Lady)* – the earliest known setting of the mass by one composer – and many other vocal works.

○ **Mahler, Gustav** (1860–1911) Austrian composer Gustav Mahler wrote some intensely romantic music, especially in his ten symphonies – the fifth is famous for its Adagietto. Mahler also composed *Song of the Earth* and *Kindertotenlieder (Songs on the Death of Children)* for singer and orchestra.

○ **Mendelssohn, Felix** (1809–47) Mendelssohn was a German composer of several well-known overtures, notably *A Midsummer Night's Dream* and *The Hebrides (or Fingal's Cave)*. He wrote five symphonies, of which the fourth (the *Italian*) is popular; *Songs Without Words* for piano; and an octet for strings. He also composed two oratorios, anthems, and some organ music.

○ **Messiaen, Olivier** (1908–92) Birdsong and Indian music provided two of this French composer's many sources of inspiration. His major works include the *Turangalîla Symphony*, *Chronochromie*, and *The Ascension* for orchestra; the chamber work *Quartet for the End of Time*, composed in a prisoner-of-war camp; *Catalogue of Birds* for piano, and *The Nativity* for organ.

○ **Monteverdi, Claudio** (1567–1643) This Italian composer wrote the first major operas – *Orpheus*, *The Return of Ulysses*, and *The Coronation of Poppaea*, in which he also developed the use of the orchestra.

○ **Mozart, Wolfgang Amadeus** (1756–91) Mozart was an Austrian composer who developed the symphony, concerto, and sonata into perfect classical forms, and also

developed opera into a highly expressive art. He composed 41 symphonies, 27 piano concertos, and 17 piano sonatas. Of these the Symphony no. 40 in G minor, Piano Concerto no. 21 in C major, and Piano Sonata no. 11 in A major (which contains the famous *Turkish Rondo*) are very popular. His concertos for the clarinet, for the flute and harp, and for the horn, are also very well known, as is the small orchestral work *Eine Kleine Nachtmusik (A Little Night Music)*. His major operas include *The Abduction from the Seraglio*, *The Marriage of Figaro*, *Don Giovanni*, *Così Fan Tutte*, and *The Magic Flute*.

○ **Mussorgsky, Modest** (1839–81) This Russian composer is known mainly for the orchestral piece *Night on Bare Mountain*, the opera *Boris Godunov*, and the piano work *Pictures at an Exhibition*, which is often played in an orchestral version by Ravel.

○ **Offenbach, Jacques** (1819–80) A French composer born in Germany, Offenbach wrote about 100 operettas – *Orpheus in the Underworld*, which contains the famous *Galop*, and *La Belle Hélène (Beautiful Helen)* are the best known. He also composed a serious and ambitious opera, *The Tales of Hoffman*, which contains the popular *Barcarolle*.

○ **Paganini, Nicolò** (1782–1840) A virtuoso violinist as well as a composer, the Italian Paganini raised violin playing to new heights. His works include 24 *Caprices* for solo violin and six violin concertos.

○ **Palestrina, Giovanni** (c.1525–94) Italian composer Palestrina wrote much church music for unaccompanied choir. He also wrote madrigals and almost 100 masses.

○ **Prez, Josquin des** (c.1440–1521) This Flemish composer wrote 18 masses, about 100 motets, and many songs. Josquin, as he is often called, is renowned for developing a new and more direct way of expressing emotions in music.

○ **Prokofiev, Sergei** (1891–1953) Prokofiev, a Russian composer, wrote modern works in classical forms. These include seven symphonies, of which no. 1 (*Classical Symphony*) is well known, and two violin concertos. He also composed the famous ballet *Romeo and Juliet*; the operas *The Love of Three Oranges* and *War and Peace*; and the orchestral works *Lieutenant Kijé* and *Peter and the Wolf*.

○ **Puccini, Giacomo** (1858–1924) An Italian composer of romantic and highly dramatic operas, Puccini composed *La Bohème*, *Tosca*, *Madame Butterfly*, and *Turandot*, which is renowned for the aria *Nessun Dorma (None Shall Sleep)*.

○ **Purcell, Henry** (1659–95) This English composer is known mainly for the opera *Dido and Aeneas*, and the theatrical work *The Fairy Queen*. He also wrote choral music for the church, and instrumental music for the English court and theater.

Olivier Messiaen

Rachmaninov, Sergei (1873–1943) A Russian composer, Rachmaninov lived in Switzerland and the United States from 1918. His highly romantic works include three symphonies and four piano concertos, of which the second is very well known. Other popular works by Rachmaninov include the *Rhapsody on a Theme of Paganini* for piano and orchestra.

Rameau, Jean-Philippe (1683–1764) A French composer of many operas and ballets, Rameau's works often use special effects to depict actions, like earthquakes, that developed the use of the orchestra

Ravel, Maurice (1875–1937) French composer Maurice Ravel often wrote music in the impressionist style. His major works include *Pavane for a Dead Princess* and *Mother Goose*, both written for piano and later orchestrated; the orchestral work *Bolero*, with its famous repetitive drum rhythm; the ballet *Daphnis and Chloe;* and two piano concertos.

Reich, Steve (b. 1936) An American composer, Reich is a key figure in the development of minimalist music. His major works include *Drumming, Different Trains, Desert Music,* and *Music for Eighteen Musicians.*

Rimsky-Korsakov, Nicolai (1844–1908) A Russian composer best known for his colorful orchestral works *Sheherazade* and *Cappriccio Espagnol (Spanish Caprice).* Rimsky-Korsakov also wrote the famous piece *Flight of the Bumble Bee.*

Rossini, Gioacchino (1792–1868) The Italian composer Rossini is famous for his often light-hearted operas, which include *The Barber of Seville, The Thieving Magpie, The Silken Ladder,* and *William Tell.*

Saint-Saëns, Camille (1835–1921) The French composer Saint-Saëns is known mainly for the orchestral entertainment *Carnival of the Animals,* which contains the famous piece *The Swan,* and the orchestral work *Danse Macabre.*

Satie, Erik (1866–1925) Born in France, Satie wrote mainly short and simple pieces, such as the well known *Three Gymnopédies.*

Scarlatti, Domenico (1685–1757) The Italian composer Scarlatti developed keyboard

Dmitri Shostakovich

music with a series of more than 550 short sonatas for the harpsichord.

Schoenberg, Arnold (1874–1951) An Austrian composer, Schoenberg lived in the United States from 1933. He first wrote romantic music, as in the string sextet *Verklärte Nacht (Transfigured Night).* He later developed atonal music, as in the vocal work *Pierrot Lunaire,* and twelve-tone or serial music, as in *Variations for Orchestra.*

Schubert, Franz (1797–1828) Schubert, an Austrian composer of lyrical and poetic music, wrote nine symphonies, of which no. 8 (*The Unfinished*) is very popular; 15 string quartets, including no. 14 (*Death and the Maiden*); and over 600 songs. The *Trout* quintet, a chamber work, and *Impromptus* for piano are also widely known.

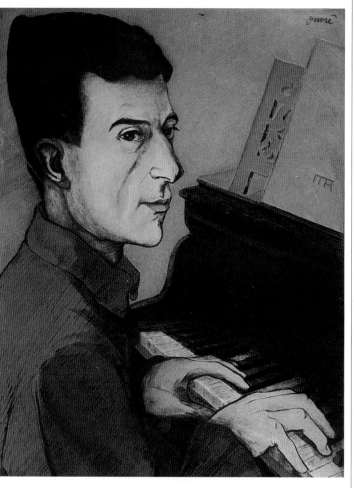

Maurice Ravel

Schumann, Robert (1810–56) A German composer of romantic music, Schumann wrote four symphonies and several concertos, of which the Piano Concerto in A minor is very popular. He also wrote a number of well-known piano works, including *Carnaval* and *Scenes from Childhood.*

Shostakovich, Dmitri (1906–75) Shostakovich was a Russian composer who wrote music mainly in classical forms, including 15 symphonies and 15 string quartets. The 8th quartet commemorates the destruction of the German city of Dresden in World War II, and is particularly moving. Shostakovich also wrote music for films, theater, and the ballet.

Sibelius, Jean (1865–1957) This Finnish composer wrote a great deal of music related to his native country, including the orchestral works *Finlandia* and *Karelia.* He also composed the well-known orchestral work *Valse Triste (Sad Waltz),* seven symphonies, and a violin concerto.

Smetana, Bedrich (1824–84) A Czech composer, Smetana wrote music in the national style of his country. This includes six symphonic poems called *Má Vlast (My Country),* of which *Vltava* is the best known. He also wrote the opera *The Bartered Bride.*

Stockhausen, Karlheinz (b. 1928) The German composer Stockhausen has explored several new ways of making music. These include total serialism, as in *Zeitmasse (Tempos)* for wind quintet; electronic music, as in *Kontakte (Contact),* and *Hymnen (Anthems);* electronic treatment of instruments, as in *Mikrophonie I* for gong; and vocal experiments, as in *Stimmung (Mood).*

Strauss, Johann (1825–99) Johann Strauss, an Austrian composer of light music, is famous for his Viennese waltzes, such as *The Blue Danube,* and operettas, of which *Die Fledermaus (The Bat)* is very popular.

Strauss, Richard (1864–1949) This German composer of 20th-century romantic music is best known for his symphonic poems, which include *Also sprach Zarathustra (Thus spake Zarathustra)* and *Till Eulenspiegel,* and his operas, which include *Elektra, Salome,* and *Der Rosenkavalier.*

Igor Stravinsky with part of the score of *The Rite of Spring*

Giuseppe Verdi

○ **Stravinsky, Igor** (1882–1971) This Russian composer spent most of his life working in Switzerland, France, and the United States. Three ballets – *The Firebird, Petrushka,* and *The Rite of Spring* – and the stage work *The Soldier's Tale,* established him as a composer of original music. He then turned to music that explored past styles, as in the ballets *Apollo* and *Pulcinella,* and the choral work *Symphony of Psalms.* Finally he adopted the twelve-tone method developed by Schoenberg. Many consider him to be the greatest composer of the 20th century.

○ **Takemitsu, Toru** (b. 1930) Japanese composer Takemitsu has written orchestral, vocal, chamber, and piano works. He has composed music that combines Japanese folk instruments with the symphony orchestra.

○ **Tchaikovsky, Peter Ilyich** (1840–93) Highly tuneful romantic music is the hallmark of Russian composer Tchaikovsky. His major works include six symphonies, of which no. 6 (*Pathétique*) is very popular; three piano concertos, the first of which is best known; a violin concerto; the orchestral works *Romeo and Juliet Fantasy Overture* and *1812 Overture;* and the ballets *Swan Lake, The Sleeping Beauty,* and *The Nutcracker.*

○ **Varèse, Edgard** (1883–1965) A French composer who lived in the United States from 1915, Varèse explored unusual sounds. He wrote *Ionisation,* a work for percussion.

○ **Vaughan Williams, Ralph** (1872–1958) A British composer who often made use of folk music, Vaughan Williams's works include *Fantasia on a Theme by Thomas Tallis* for strings, nine symphonies, and the song cycle *On Wenlock Edge.*

○ **Verdi, Giuseppe** (1813–1901) This Italian composer is best known for his dramatic operas, such as *Rigoletto, Il Trovatore (The Troubadour), La Traviata, The Force of Destiny, Aida, Otello,* and *Falstaff.*

○ **Villa-Lobos, Heitor** (1887–1959) The Brazilian composer Villa-Lobos is known for *Bachianas Brasilieras,* nine works that express the spirit of J.S. Bach in Brazilian style. No. 5 for soprano and eight cellos is famous.

○ **Vivaldi, Antonio** (1678–1741) This Italian composer developed the concerto with about 350 works for a solo instrument and orchestra. The best known is the set of four violin concertos called *The Four Seasons.*

○ **Wagner, Richard** (1813–83) German composer Richard Wagner greatly developed opera, harmony, and orchestration with his highly dramatic music dramas. These include *The Flying Dutchman, Tannhäuser, Lohengrin, The Mastersingers of Nuremberg,* and *The Ring of the Nibelungen* cycle (*The Rhinegold, The Valkyrie, Siegfried,* and *Twilight of the Gods*).

○ **Weill, Kurt** (1900–50) Weill was a German composer of stage works who lived in the United States from 1935. His major works are *The Threepenny Opera* (which has the famous song *Mack the Knife*), *Happy End,* and *The Rise and Fall of the City of Mahagonny.*

Musical forms

Sweet Honey-sucking Bees is a madrigal by John Wilbye

o Anthem A short religious work for choir. An anthem is often accompanied by an organ and performed as part of a church service.
•*Zadok The Priest* by Handel
•*Thou Wilt Keep Him in Splendid Peace* by Samuel Wesley

o Aria A song for one singer accompanied by an orchestra. The principal performers in an opera or the soloists in an oratorio sing arias. These are full compositions, containing a strong melody, which express feelings or actions at that specific point in the story of the opera or oratorio.
•*I Know That My Redeemer Liveth* from *Messiah* by Handel
•*The Bird-catcher* and *I'll have Revenge* from *The Magic Flute* by Mozart
•*Your Tiny Hand is Frozen* from *La Bohème* by Puccini

Papageno is the comic bird-catcher in *The Magic Flute*, an opera by Mozart

o Cadenza Part of a movement in a concerto in which the soloist plays alone to exhibit his or her virtuosity. Early concertos have a space set aside for a cadenza, which is either improvised (made up by the soloist on the spot) or composed by the soloist or another musician. In later concertos, the cadenza is written by the composer of the concerto.
•Cadenza in first movement of Violin Concerto in D major by Beethoven; the soloist often plays a cadenza composed by the great violinist, Fritz Kreisler
•Cadenza in first movement of Piano Concerto in A minor by Grieg (composed by Grieg)

o Cantata A work for choir or chorus and (usually) an orchestra; there may also be solo singers. Early cantatas have one or more solo singers and some do not have a chorus.
•Cantata no. 147 by J.S. Bach (contains the chorale *Jesu, Joy of Man's Desiring*)
•*Hiawatha* by Samuel Coleridge-Taylor
•*Carmina Burana* by Carl Orff

o Coda A section that concludes a movement of a piece of music. It often comes after the last appearance of the main theme.

o Concerto A long piece of music, usually in several movements, for a solo instrument and an orchestra. It shows how brilliantly the soloist can play. A "concerto for orchestra" has no soloist and is a display piece for an orchestra.
•Clarinet Concerto in A major by Mozart
•Violin Concerto in E minor by Mendelssohn
•Piano Concerto no. 1 in B-flat minor by Tchaikovsky
•Cello Concerto in B minor by Dvořák
•*Concierto de Aranjuez* (for guitar) by Joaquin Rodrigo
•Concerto for Orchestra by Bartók

o Concerto grosso A concerto for a group of players instead of one soloist.
•Brandenburg Concerto no. 2 (for trumpet, recorder, oboe, and violin) by J.S. Bach

o Etude See Study

o Fugue A piece of music for a certain number of parts, in which one part starts with a tune and then the other parts enter one by one with the same tune. The parts then continue to imitate each other and intertwine as they develop the tune or introduce new tunes. The parts may be separate voices or instruments, or all the parts may be played on a keyboard.
•Fugue no. 5 from Book I of *The Well-Tempered Clavier* by J.S. Bach
•*Cat's Fugue* by Domenico Scarlatti
•*Great Fugue* by Beethoven
•Fugue from *The Young Person's Guide to the Orchestra* by Britten

o Impromptu A short piece of music, usually for a piano. Though completely written down, it suggests that the performer is so inspired as to be making the music up on the spot.
•Impromptu in G flat major by Schubert
•*Fantasie-Impromptu* by Chopin

o Lieder Songs for one singer, accompanied usually by a piano but sometimes by an orchestra. Lieder are often settings of poems. A single song is called a Lied, and groups of songs are known as song cycles.
•*Who is Sylvia?*, *The Erl-King*, *Gretchen at the Spinning Wheel*, and *The Trout*, all by Schubert

o Madrigal A piece of music for several singers, in which each singer has a separate part and may sing different words from the other singers. Madrigals are usually settings of poems, often about love and rarely religious. They are early works, dating from the 14th to 17th centuries, and are usually sung unaccompanied. Madrigals are also sung by choirs.
•*Sweet Honey-sucking Bees* and *Adieu, Sweet Amaryllis* by John Wilbye
•*O Care Thou Wilt Despatch Me* by Thomas Weelkes
•*The Silver Swan* by Orlando Gibbons

o Mass A religious choral work consisting of a setting of the Roman Catholic service, also called the Mass.
•*Missa L'Homme Armé* by Palestrina
•Mass in B minor by J.S. Bach
•*Missa Solemnis* or Mass in D by Beethoven

o Minuet A dance in triple meter that became an instrumental piece in the 18th century – especially the third movement of a symphony, sonata, or string quartet. It often contains a middle section called a trio.
•Third movement of Symphony no. 40 in G minor by Mozart
•Minuet in G for piano by Beethoven

Motet An early work, usually for singers, but also for instruments, dating from the 13th to 17th centuries. It takes an existing melody and words to which other melodies and words are added. A motet is also a short work for choir, often accompanied by an organ and performed in church.
•*Ave Maria Gratia Plena* by Josquin des Prez
•*Spem in Alium* by Thomas Tallis
•*Singet dem Herrn* by J.S. Bach
•*Exsultate, Jubilate* by Mozart

Movement A section of a long work, such as a symphony, concerto, string quartet, or sonata; these longer works are usually divided into three, four, or five movements, which are complete pieces of music in themselves played at different tempos (speeds). There is normally a short break between each movement, though sometimes two movements may be played without a break. The movements may have Italian names such as "adagio" or "presto," which indicate their speed, or titles that are musical forms, such as "minuet" or "rondo." The last movement of a piece is often called the "finale."

Nocturne A short piano piece with a quiet reflective mood. Nocturne means "night piece," and the title has occasionally been used for atmospheric orchestral works.
•Nocturne in E-flat major by Chopin
•*Nocturnes* by Debussy

Oratorio A large work for a big choir or chorus or even two choirs, several solo singers, and an orchestra. The words are often religious and may be settings of Bible stories. Oratorios are performed in churches as well as concert halls, usually without costumes and scenery.
•*Messiah* by Handel
•*The Creation* by Haydn
•*Elijah* by Mendelssohn
•*A Child of our Time* by Michael Tippett

Overture A short orchestral piece that precedes the opening scene of an opera or a play. A concert overture is a short orchestral piece often played at the beginning of a concert; it may describe a scene or event in musical terms.
•Overture to *The Barber of Seville* by Rossini
•*The Hebrides* by Mendelssohn
•*1812 Overture* by Tchaikovsky

Passion An oratorio based on the Biblical story of the suffering, death, and resurrection of Jesus Christ.
•*St. Matthew Passion* by J.S. Bach

•*St. John Passion* by J.S. Bach
•*St. Luke Passion* by Krzysztof Penderecki

Prelude A short piece that introduces another piece, as in a prelude and fugue. Also a short piece in its own right, usually for piano solo but sometimes for orchestra.
•Prelude no. 1 from Book I of *The Well-Tempered Clavier* by J.S. Bach
•Prelude no. 15 (*Raindrop Prelude*) by Chopin
•Prelude in C-sharp minor by Rachmaninov
•*The Girl with the Flaxen Hair* from Preludes by Debussy

Program music Music intended to portray a subject, such as scenery, a painting, a historical event like a battle, or a story. Program music is not a musical form in itself; forms such as symphonies and overtures that portray a subject, are said to be program music.

Rimsky-Korsakov's *Sheherazade* is based on tales from the *Arabian Nights*

•*The Four Seasons* by Vivaldi
•*Pictures at an Exhibition* by Mussorgsky
•*Carnival of the Animals* by Saint-Saëns
•*Sheherazade* by Rimsky-Korsakov
•*The Sorcerer's Apprentice* by Paul Dukas
•*La Mer* (*The Sea*) by Debussy
•*An American in Paris* by Gershwin
•*The Little Train* by Villa-Lobos

Recitative A piece in an opera or oratorio in which a singer recites the words, often by singing them mostly on one note, with a simple accompaniment. A recitative enables a singer to perform a spoken passage, and it often comes before a song.

Requiem A choral work sung in memory of the dead. It may be a musical setting of the Roman Catholic Mass for the dead, and is performed in concert halls and churches.
•*A German Requiem* by Brahms
•Requiem by Verdi
•Requiem by Fauré
•*War Requiem* by Britten

Rhapsody A title intended to suggest that the music is imaginative and inspired. A rhapsody is usually an instrumental composition, and it does not have a particular musical form. For

example, *Rhapsody on a Theme by Paganini* by Rachmaninov is a theme and variations.
•Hungarian Rhapsody no. 2 in C-sharp minor by Liszt
•*Alto Rhapsody* by Brahms
•Rhapsody for Saxophone and Orchestra by Debussy
•*Rhapsody in Blue* by Gershwin

Rondo A piece of music in which the same tune occurs several times, but in between each appearance there is a contrasting episode of some other music. The last movement of a sonata or concerto is often in rondo form.

•*Gypsy Rondo* from Piano Trio no. 1 in G major by Haydn
•*Turkish Rondo* from Piano Sonata no. 11 in A major by Mozart
•Rondo from Horn Concerto no. 4 in E-flat major by Mozart

Scherzo A lively movement in a long work such as a symphony or string quartet, often replacing the minuet in such a work. Like the minuet, a scherzo contains a middle section called a trio. Scherzo is also a name for a lively piece in its own right.
•Third movement of Symphony no. 5 in C minor by Beethoven
•Scherzo no. 2 by Chopin

Serenade Originally a piece of music intended for evening performance in the open air, but later a general title of no particular significance.
•Serenade no. 10 in B-flat major for 13 Wind Instruments and Double Bass, and *Eine Kleine Nachtmusik (A Little Night Music)*, both by Mozart
•Serenade for Flute, Violin, and Viola by Beethoven
•Serenade for Strings by Tchaikovsky
•Serenade for Tenor, Horn, and Strings by Britten

The firebird, from Stravinsky's ballet of the same name

○ **Sonata** Originally a piece of music that is played rather than sung, but mainly a long work for one or two instruments in several movements. The first movement is usually in sonata form, and the last movement a lively rondo. In between come a slow movement and often a minuet. A piano sonata is for the piano only. In a violin or cello sonata, a piano accompanies the violin or cello.
•Piano Sonata no. 15 in C major (*Easy Sonata*) by Mozart
•Sonata no. 8 in C minor (*Pathétique Sonata*) by Beethoven
•Sonata no. 14 in C-sharp minor (*Moonlight Sonata*) by Beethoven
•Violin Sonata in A minor (*Kreutzer Sonata*) by Beethoven

○ **Sonata form** A standard form for the first movement and sometimes other movements of an instrumental work, including the symphony and concerto as well as the sonata itself. It consists of three main sections – an exposition in which two themes or tunes are stated, a development section in which the themes are reworked and expanded in various ways, and a recapitulation in which the opening themes appear again, often modified in some way.

○ **Song cycle** A group of songs performed in a particular order, in which the singer is accompanied by a piano or an orchestra. The words may come from a group of poems and, in their entirety, may tell a story.
•*Winter's Journey* by Schubert
•*Sea Pictures* by Elgar
•*Songs on the Death of Children* by Mahler

○ **Study or Etude** A short piece, usually for one instrument, intended as an exercise in a particular way of playing.
•*100 Progressive Studies* by Carl Czerny
•*Etude no. 12 in C minor (Revolutionary Study)* by Chopin

○ **Suite** An instrumental piece in several short movements. In suites of the 17th and 18th centuries, the movements make up a set of dances (usually an allemande, courante, sarabande, gigue, minuet, gavotte, and bourrée) sometimes preceded by an overture. A suite is also a collection of orchestral pieces taken from a long work, usually a ballet or opera, and performed on their own without any dancing or singing. The pieces are played without a break, and often consist of the principal tunes in the long work.
•Cello Suite no. 3 by J.S. Bach
•Orchestral Suite no. 3 (contains *Air for the G String*) by J.S. Bach
•*Music for the Royal Fireworks* by Handel
•*Children's Games* by Bizet
•*Nutcracker Suite* by Tchaikovsky
•*The Firebird Suite* by Stravinsky

Dohnányi wrote a set of variations on the nursery rhyme, *Twinkle, Twinkle Little Star*

○ **Symphonic poem or Tone poem** A long orchestral work, often in a single continuous movement, in which the music portrays a subject such as a historical or fictional character, a story, a landscape, or a mythological theme.
•*Hamlet* by Liszt
•*Vltava* from *Má Vlast (My Country)* by Smetana
•*Thus Spake Zarathustra* by Richard Strauss
•*Don Quixote* by Richard Strauss

○ **Symphony** A long work for orchestra, sometimes including a chorus and solo singers, in several movements. A symphony usually has the same structure as a sonata, often having four movements, the first of which is in sonata form. But

the orchestra gives the symphony a much greater contrast of sound.
•Symphony no. 3 in E-flat major (*Eroica Symphony*) by Beethoven
•Symphony no. 8 in B minor (*Unfinished Symphony*) by Schubert
•Symphony no. 9 in E minor (*From the New World*) by Dvorák
•Symphony no. 6 in B minor (*Pathétique*) by Tchaikovsky
•*Symphony of Psalms* by Stravinsky

○ **Theme and variations** A piece of music that begins with a particular theme or tune, which is then repeated several times but changed or varied in some way. Each variation is different. Some may resemble the original theme, while in others the notes are changed so that they sound quite unlike the original theme.
•*Goldberg Variations* by J.S. Bach
•Piano Sonata no. 11 in A major by Mozart
•*Variations on a Theme of Haydn (St. Anthony Chorale)* by Brahms
•*Variations on a Nursery Song* by Dohnányi
•*Variations on America* by Charles Ives
•*Enigma Variations* by Elgar

○ **Toccata** A fast and dazzling piece for one instrument designed to show off the performer's ability.
•Toccata and Fugue in D minor by J.S. Bach
•Toccata from Fifth Organ Symphony by Charles-Marie Widor

○ **Tone poem** See Symphonic Poem

○ **Variation** See Theme and variations

○ **Waltz or Valse** A dance in triple time (three beats to the bar) that was very popular in the 19th century. There are many waltzes for piano or orchestra that are played as pieces of music for listening rather than dancing.
•*Grande Valse Brillante* from a collection of 15 Waltzes by Chopin
•*Tales from the Vienna Woods* and *The Blue Danube* by Johann Strauss
•*La Valse* by Ravel

The waltz

Glossary of musical terms

Words in *italics* have their own entry in this glossary.

accompaniment Music that accompanies or supports singers or instruments having a leading role.

adagio An instruction to play a piece or part of a piece of music slowly.

allegro An instruction to play a piece or part of a piece of music fast.

alto A voice of medium-high range, or an instrument of medium-high pitch in a group of related instruments. Alto is below *soprano* and above *tenor*.

andante An instruction to play a piece or part of a piece of music at medium speed.

baritone A male voice of low range or a low instrument in a group of related instruments. Baritone is below *tenor* and above *bass*.

bass Low in *pitch*. Also, the male voice with the lowest range, or usually the lowest instrument in a range of instruments. Bass is below *baritone*.

bend Make a note go *flat*

chord A group of notes that are all played at the same time.

clef A sign at the beginning of a *staff* that indicates the pitch of the staff's five lines and four spaces. The *treble* clef 𝄞 is used for high instruments and voices, the *alto* or *tenor* clef 𝄡 for medium instruments and voices, and the bass clef 𝄢 for low instruments and voices.

counterpoint The combination of two or more separate *melodies*, the notes of which sound against each other to produce a pleasant *harmony*.

crescendo An instruction to make the music get louder.

flat A note that is one *semitone* lower in *pitch* than a *natural* note – for example, B-flat is one semitone lower than B. A note that sounds slightly lower than it should be is also said to be flat.

harmony The sound produced when two or more notes of different *pitch* sound together. Some notes give a pleasant harmony, while others sound discordant.

improvise To make up music as it is being played or sung, instead of playing or singing composed music.

largo An instruction to play a piece or part of a piece of music slowly.

key (1) The first and last *note* of a *major* or *minor scale*. A scale may be in the key of G major, for example, meaning that the scale begins and ends on the note of G. The title of a piece of music often includes the key, as in Mozart's Symphony no. 40 in G minor – this means that the music starts with notes in the scale of G minor, though it usually then moves to other keys before returning to the opening key at the end of the piece.

key (2) A lever on a wind or keyboard instrument that is operated by a finger to produce a sound.

major A *scale*, *key*, *harmony*, or *chord* containing a set of *notes* that often give a cheerful sound. For example, the sequence of notes C, D, E, F, G, A, B, C give a scale in the key of C major, and the group of notes C, E, G give a C major chord. Major scales and major chords in other keys have the same relative distance between the notes.

melody A tune or *theme* made up of a sequence of notes with a distinctive musical line.

minor A *scale*, *key*, *harmony*, or *chord* containing a set of *notes* that often give a sad sound. For example, the sequence of notes C, D, E-flat, F, G, A-flat, B-flat, C give a scale in the key of C minor, and the group of notes C, E-flat, G give a C minor chord. Minor scales and minor chords in other keys have the same relative distance between the notes.

natural A note that is neither a *flat* nor a *sharp*. The white keys on the piano are natural notes.

notation The way in which music is written down, usually on a *staff*.

note A single sound having a particular *pitch* and lasting for a certain time.

octave A span of eight *notes*, beginning and ending on a note having the same letter name – for example, the distance between one F-sharp and the next (up or down) is an octave.

opus (op.) Latin word meaning "work," used with a number to identify a particular work in a complete catalog of a composer's music.

orchestration The way in which a composer uses the instruments in writing music for an orchestra.

part An individual line of music in a piece made up of several lines, as in a three-part fugue, or vocal music in four parts for *soprano*, *alto*, *tenor*, and *bass*. Also the piece of written music that an individual chamber or orchestral player uses, such as the flute part.

pitch The highness or lowness of a particular *note*. The twelve notes of the chromatic *scale* give different sensations of pitch from each other. However, all notes in *octaves*, such as all the G keys on a piano, give a similar sensation of pitch.

polyphonic Music which comprises a number of different melodic lines that sound simultaneously.

presto An instruction to play a piece or part of a piece of music very fast.

register A part of the complete range of *notes* produced by an instrument or voice with its own distinctive sound, such as the high register or the low register.

rhythm The lengths of the *notes* in a piece of music. The rhythm may be even, with notes having the same length. Most music has rhythms with notes of different lengths, but often in repeated patterns. Rhythmic music is music in which the rhythm is emphasized, helping to give it energy and make it dance.

scale A basic sequence of *notes* used to create *melody* and *harmony* in a piece of music. In *major* and *minor* scales, there are eight notes in all. A chromatic scale contains all the 13 notes in the *octave*, such as A, A-sharp, B, C, C-sharp, D, D-sharp, E, F, F-sharp, G, G-sharp, and A.

semitone The smallest step between one *note* and another. C-sharp is a semitone above C, for example.

sharp A *note* that is one *semitone* higher in *pitch* than another note, so that F-sharp is higher than F, for example. A note that is sung or played slightly higher than it should be is said to be sharp.

solo Playing or singing alone, or as a featured instrumentalist or singer with an orchestra or choir. A solo performer is called a soloist.

soprano The female voice with the highest range, or usually the highest instrument in a range of instruments. Soprano is above *alto*.

staff The set of five lines on and around which music is written. Also called a stave.

tempo The speed at which a piece of music is played or sung.

tenor A male voice with a medium-low range, or an instrument of medium-low pitch in a group of related instruments. Tenor is below *alto* and above *baritone*.

theme A *melody*, or a short sequence of *notes*, on which a piece of music is based.

tonal Music that is in a particular *key*, or which changes from one key to another. Tonal music often has the sense of moving toward certain home *note* or key, on which it may end.

tone The kind of sound produced by an instrument or the sound of a definite pitch.

treble High in pitch.

tuning Adjusting the *pitch* of the *notes* produced by an instrument so that they are the same as a standard pitch, often given by a tuning fork. The instrument is then "in tune." Instruments that play together must be in tune with each other.

virtuoso A performer who can sing or play with great skill or "virtuosity."

Index

Acknowledgments

Dorling Kindersley would like to thank:
Peter Hewitt and Ian Fowler (Royal College of Music) and the following students from the Royal College of Music Junior Department – Alex Comninos, Augusta Harris, Elizabeth Park, Toby Gillman, Sally Pryce, Michael East, Jonathan Gow, Sara Temple, Alison Jury, Luke Bedford, Vian Sharif, Elisabeth Griffin, Howard Beagley, Ewan Davenport, Daisy Reid, Jane Stoneham, Tim Gunnell, Sebastian Ferreira, Sam Walton, Alison Cooke, Sarah Partridge, Stephen Russell, and James Slater. Nicholas Tollervey. Kwasi Kufuor. Nancy Graham. Elizabeth de la Porte, Elizabeth Page, and Jane Chapman (Royal College of Music). The Rev'd D.B. Tillyer and Mr Ian Shaw (St. Peter's Church, Eaton Square). Argent's music shop. Rolf Hind and Ray Rowden. Rosemary Johnson (Chester Music). Louise Badger and Kate Finch (BBC Symphony Orchestra). Sylvia Potter for the index.

Illustrator: David Ashby

Picture credits: l=left; r= right; t = top; c = center; b = bottom.

AKG, London 67tl; 68tr; 74br; /Florence, Cabinetto Disegno e Stampe 58tl. J. Allan Cash Photolibrary 62cr. Ancient Art and Architecture Collection 55tl; 56cra; 57c; 57r; 60tr. BBC Photolibrary 69bl. Beethoven-Archiv, Bonn 17bc. Boosey & Hawkes 67cra. Bridgeman Art Library, London/Aberdeen Art Gallery & Museum, *Pope I*, © The Francis Bacon Estate, 68l; /Bibliothèque Nationale, Paris/Artothek, *Ravel at the Piano* 1911, Achille Ouvre 74br; /Bibliothèque Nationale, Paris/Giraudon, MS Fr. 12476 f. 98 *Martin Le France, Le Champion des Dames* 57cla; /Bonhams, London, *Study for a Figure of a Dancer For Scheherazade*, Leon Bakst 77cr; /British Library, London, AD 27696 F. 13 *Ruler enthroned with attendants* 55bl; /Crown Estate/Institute of Directors, London, *King William III*, Sir Godfrey Kneller 17tcl; Crown Estate/Institute of Directors, London, *Queen Mary*, Sir Godfrey Kneller 17tcr; /Fitzwilliam Museum, University of Cambridge, *Scheherazade Costume Design*, Leon Bakst 77cl; /Historisches Museum der Stadt, Vienna, *A Schubert Evening at the House of Joseph V. Spaun*, Moritz von Schwind 60br; /Lauros-Giraudon/Chateau de Versailles, *Bonaparte Crossing the Alps*, Jacques Louis David 17br; /Leamington Spa Museum & Art Gallery, Warwickshire, *The Dream from the Bluebird*, 1911, Frederick Cayley Robinson 78c; /Louvre, Paris, *The Cello Lesson*, 58bl; /Mozart Museum, Salzburg/Giraudon, *String Quartet*, Anonymous 48bl; /Musée de l'Opera, Paris, *Tamara Karsavina as the Firebird (by Stravinsky)*, Jacques-Emile Blanche, © DACS 1995 78tl; /Museum für Geschichte de Stadt, Leipzig, *Gottfried Reiche (1667-1734)* 58br; /Museu Sorolla, Madrid/Index, *Granada*, 1920, Joaquin y Bastida Sorolla, © DACS 1995 67cl; /Prado Museum, Madrid, *The Ommeganck, Brussels, Procession of Notre Dame de Sablon*, 58tr; /Private Collection, *The Concert*, Master of The Female Half Lengths 57bl; /Private Collection, *Debussy at the Piano*, Jacques-Emile Blanche, © DACS 1995 71br; /Private Collection, *French Ballet Costume for a Eunuch, Scheherazade*, Leon Bakst 77cl. Camera Press 74tc; 44br; /Bildermanas 69tl. Malcolm Crowthers 69cra. Decca Records 71tr. C.M. Dixon 54c; 54cl. Dominic Photography/Catherine Ashmore 64bc. Editions Leduc, Paris/UMP Ltd 73c. E.T. Archive18bl; 60 bl; /Museo Bibiografico, Bologna 61cla; /Private Collection 72br; /Museum der Stadt, Vienna 78br. Mary Evans Picture Library 16bl; 54blr; 56l; 56br; 56tr; 57br; 57tl; 57br; 59 cl; 60cr; 61cl; 60cb; 62tl; 62cb; 63tr; 63tl; 63cl; 63br; 64br; 64cr; 65br; 65cl; 67tr; 70c; 76bl. The Ronald Grant Archive 17tr; 69tc. Robert Harding Picture Library/Larsen-Collings 60tc. The Hulton-Deutsch Collection 59ct; 61bl; 66bl; 66tl; 70; 72tc; 72bl; 75. Michael Holford 55c; /British Museum 54cra; 54tc. Alex von Koettlitz 11br. Lies Askonas Ltd/Keith Saunders Photography 33bl. The Mansell Collection 10bl; 16tr; 40bl; 58c; 61tr; 64tr. Performing Arts Library/Clive Barda 17cla; 17cl; 26tr; 43br; 46tr; /Susan Benn 11br. Photostage/Donald Cooper 61bl; 62bl; 62br; 63br; 64l; 65cra; 66bl; 66br; 67bc; 69cl. Pictor International 69tc. Popperfoto 68cr. Range/Bettman Archive 71br; 71br. Redferns/Susan Benn 11br; /Malcolm Crowthers 68br; 69cr; /Suzy Gibbons 69br; /David Redfern 27br; 41tr; /Bob Willoughby 49tr. REX Features Ltd 37tr. Schott Universal Music Publishers 69tr. Tony Stone Images/Robert Everts 65c; /Len Nisnevich 66c. Werner Forman Archive/C.K. Chan, Hong Kong 54bc. ZEFA/R. Bond 16br.

Every effort has been made to trace the copyright holders. Dorling Kindersley apologizes for any unintentional omissions and would be pleased, in such cases, to add an acknowledgment in future editions.